MW00606284

"Personal, perceptive, provocative, pleasurable to peruse, and those are y~~
the P's! Michael Lucker's *Crash! Boom! Bang!* is an authentic contribution
to the expanding body of screenwriting literature. Designed in particular
for writers of action/adventure fare, there are keen insights here and tons
of worthy advice also for writers of dramatic narratives in any genre."
—PROF. RICHARD WALTER, UCLA Screenwriting Chairman

"You don't have to be a writer of action films to benefit from Michael
Lucker's rock-solid screenwriting advice, but if you are an action writer…
it is essential."
—JOHN BALDECCHI, Producer: *Point Break, The Mexican, Conan the
Barbarian*

"The knowledge Michael Lucker shares in this book is not that of an
outsider looking in, but rather an insider reaching out to all those who are
interested in learning and giving them insightful and practical information."
—ANDY FICKMAN, Director, Writer, Producer: *The Game Plan, Parental
Guidance, Paul Blart: Mall Cop 2*

"With *Crash! Boom! Bang!* Michael Lucker brings together his vast life
experience, insuppressible passion for teaching, and mastery of the screenwriting craft. This powerhouse of a book is an absolute pleasure to read.
Here, Michael entertains, he teaches, and he beckons both novice and
expert alike to excel at the craft and business of screenwriting."
—MICHAEL NORTON, Nine-time Emmy Award–winning Producer for
The Amazing Race

"*Crash! Boom! Bang!* is an indispensable how-to book peppered with the
author's personal experience going from wide-eyed wannabe to successful
scribe. Screenwriters of all stripes should read this."
—CARTER BLANCHARD, Screenwriter: DreamWorks, Warner Bros., 20th
Century Fox, New Line Cinema, Sony Pictures, Universal Pictures, Walt
Disney Pictures, and Paramount Pictures

"No one explains story structure better than Michael Lucker. In *Crash!
Boom! Bang!*, Lucker draws on his own screenwriting experiences as well
as classic action films to illustrate how to write a winning script. Lucker
combines witty, fun-to-read examples with step-by-step instructions that
lay out the basics for beginners while giving old hands some exciting new
strategies."
—DR. DONNA LITTLE, Professor and Director, MFA in Creative Writing,
Reinhardt University

"With his unique experience and keen understanding of his craft, Michael Lucker reveals step-by-step how action-packed tales are intelligently and skillfully woven. His passion is real, his integrity genuine, and his guidance witty and warm, as if from the pen of a caring mentor. If you are serious about writing an action movie... *Crash! Boom! Bang!* is a must."
—MAJ. THOMAS A. ROSS, U.S. Army Special Forces, Retired; Author of *Privileges of War*

"When it comes to action films, Michael Lucker has literally written the book on them! Whether you've had a hit movie, made a big spec sale, or have yet to type 'Fade In:' this book will teach you something you didn't know, or teach you a better way of doing something you thought you knew."
—JIM WEDAA, Producer: *The Boy, Unstoppable, Big Trouble, Mission to Mars, Black Dog*

"An exceptional and hilarious instruction manual on the craft of screenwriting, told by one of the Hollywood elite."
—NATHAN GOODMAN, Author: *The Special Agent Jana Baker Spy-Thriller Series*

"Straightforward, witty, smart, and informative. Michael Lucker's *Crash! Boom! Bang!* offers writers of action movies a hands-on manual for not only delivering on the promises of the genre, but elevating them."
—MIREILLE SORIA, Producer: *Madagascar I, II & III, Captain Underpants: The First Epic Movie, Home, Sinbad: Legend of the High Seas, Spirit: Stallion of the Cimarron, Ever After*

"With its appropriate mix of encouragement and realism, this book reads so effortlessly you'll fly through it—and yet, Lucker's insights into the craft take root and stay with you. You'll be inspired to go write and put the lessons into action."
—DR. JEFF MARKER, Associate Professor of Film, Chair of the Communication, Media & Journalism Department, University of North Georgia

"Michael Lucker's screenwriting guide reads like an action-movie script. This fun and lively page-turner is full of verve, drive, wit, insight, and inspiration. I recommend it highly!"
—DR. MATTHEW H. BERNSTEIN, Goodrich C. White Professor, Chair of the Department of Film and Media Studies, Emory University

CRASH! BOOM! BANG!

HOW TO WRITE ACTION MOVIES

MICHAEL LUCKER

MICHAEL WIESE PRODUCTIONS

Published by Michael Wiese Productions
12400 Ventura Blvd. #1111
Studio City, CA 91604
(818) 379-8799, (818) 986-3408 (FAX)
mw@mwp.com
www.mwp.com

Cover design by Johnny Ink. www.johnnyink.com
Interior design by William Morosi
Copyediting by Gary Sunshine
Printed by McNaughton & Gunn

Manufactured in the United States of America
Copyright 2017 by Michael Lucker

All rights reserved. No part of this book may be reproduced in any form or by any means without permission in writing from the author, except for the inclusion of brief quotations in a review.

Library of Congress Cataloging-in-Publication Data

Names: Lucker, Michael, author.
Title: CRASH! BOOM! BANG! : how to write action movies / Michael Lucker.
Description: Studio City, CA : Michael Wiese Productions, [2017]
Identifiers: LCCN 2017001636 | ISBN 9781615932634
Subjects: LCSH: Motion picture authorship--Handbooks, manuals, etc.
Classification: LCC PN1996 .L76 2017 | DDC 808.2/3--dc23
LC record available at https://lccn.loc.gov/2017001636

Printed on Recycled Stock

CONTENTS

FOREWORD

I admit it. I was a nudge. But who could blame me? I was a sixteen-year-old wannabe filmmaker in the suburbs of Connecticut wanting desperately to break into Hollywood. Who cared about high school? I just wanted to make movies, just like my hero, Steven Spielberg. So I wrote him a letter. And sent him my film. And called. And kept calling. To my surprise, someone in his office actually responded. It was Michael Lucker.

Despite working fourteen hours a day as Steven's production assistant, trying to write his own screenplays, and occasionally stopping to eat, Michael took time to reach out to a teenager he didn't even know a world away. Over time he watched my high school films, gave me advice on storytelling, and even wrote a letter of recommendation for me to USC Film School, where I was accepted.

Who does that?

Soon Michael's career as a screenwriter took off and I figured I'd be left in the dust. After all, when most screenwriters first get attention, they become consumed by their own careers. They have to be. Michael was meeting with movie stars, writing action movies back to back, and, well, having me over to his house to help shake off rejections of my college films.

Who does that?

It's never been about him. Or about me, for that matter. Michael's helped so many aspiring writers over the years. I think that's why he actually tells stories himself. To help others. To inspire others. To thrill others.

I remember when he was making his first big studio film. He was crazed with the usual production rewrites, but somehow made time to read my first attempt at a screenplay, which clocked in around two hundred pages. Still, he read it all.

Who the hell does that?

For years Michael's been writing movies — studio films, indie films, adaptations, you name it. And now he's passing along that experience to the rest of us. I wish there were more books like this when I was getting started. Rarely do you get to read honest stories about filmmakers in the trenches. And not just what they know about the craft and the business, but how they got there in the first place. The challenges, the victories, the disasters.

Michael does that.

Since we met, he has helped me become a better writer, director, and producer. I know the lessons in this book will help you, too, no matter where you are in your film journey, for he has a way with words that dares us all to dream, to tell our own stories and to believe we can succeed.

Luke Greenfield
Director/Writer/Producer
Let's Be Cops
Role Models
The Girl Next Door

INTRODUCTION

I was an idiot. It was sixth grade at Montgomery Elementary and I had the smallest of parts in the school play *South Pacific*. I had the monumental task of stepping onto stage with a hairbrush and delivering two lines. That was it. But I forgot the brush and I forgot my lines. In front of about 150 drop-jawed parents. So I made something up. They laughed. So I made something else up. They laughed again. Afterward I was heralded a genius and carted off on shoulders for pizza and seltzer. That was the day I realized a) I couldn't act, b) I could write. This was born out of necessity. I wasn't as cute as the cute boys in school, but I liked girls just as much. It was obvious that making them laugh made them swoon, so I decided to be funny. Right then. Right there. Before math class. Of course, I wasn't funny for quite some time, but slowly, shakily, I figured out how to move an audience. Of sixth-grade girls.

In high school, it was much the same. I wasn't as cool as the cool kids, but I could make them laugh too. Someone suggested I write funny articles about them in the school paper. So I did. Suddenly, people who never knew I existed were passing me in the hall saying how great the articles were. Mostly the drama teacher, Mr. Murray. He asked if I wanted to

write a play for the drama club to perform. *A play.* I knew no better, so I said "Sure." It was a dark comedy about a group of patients at an insane asylum who drove the staff crazy. Three hundred people came. And they laughed too. So I decided to go off to college to study writing somewhere they could train me to earn the favor of the cute girls and the cool kids.

Boston University's esteemed College of Communication had an essay component to their application. I figured whoever was reading those pages all day had to be bored out of their mind. So I wrote jokes… making fun of the application process. I got in. Hooah. They had a film and broadcasting major, and I had a dream.

Boston was a different planet. It seemed like I was the only kid in the city from south of the Mason-Dixon line. I talked different, dressed different. Think I even walked different from everyone else. Desperate to fit in, I did what I always did and started writing. Skits and songs and films and commercials. Anything to win hearts and minds in a brave new world and avoid getting my ass kicked by the Long Island student mafia. To the college's credit, they believed their writing graduates should actually have something to write about. So I had to take a wide variety of classes. I fought my way through marketing, clawed my way through astronomy, bullshitted my way through psychology. And then it happened. I took Dr. John Kelly's screenwriting class. It was like a light went on over my head. The light flashed "Do this." I thought, *Really? I can make a living doing this?* It was the most fun I ever had. And Dr. Kelly made it so. His quick wit and disarming intellect made the writing process easily digestible and inspired us all to tell our stories to the world.

After college I landed green and penniless on a couch in Pasadena ready to break into Hollywood. I got my car towed, my car stolen, my car jacked. Finally, I got my foot in the door. It got stepped on a few times, but eventually I found myself working with some of the greatest minds in the film industry — as production assistant to Steven Spielberg, creative assistant at Hollywood Pictures, and screenwriter for Disney, DreamWorks, Paramount, Fox, and Universal. I also read the books and took the seminars of some of the best screenwriting instructors in the land upon whose shoulders I now stand.

After years of triumphs and travails writing, I returned to the hills and trees of my hometown, Atlanta, which has since become a thriving hub of film production. Here I write and consult on feature films and teach screenwriting at University of North Georgia, Emory University, and in my own workshops at Screenwriter School. Thanks to the encouragement and cajoling from family, friends, and students, I now pass along the lessons I've learned in hopes they will inspire others.

What follows are my two cents on writing action movies: concept, character, plot, scene, format, action, dialogue, transition, process, rewriting, feedback, and business. Each chapter begins with an anecdote from my path as a writer and ends with a movie I recommend that exemplifies the topic within. Along the way, I hope you find something that moves you, entertains you, and, most of all, educates you. If not, I hope it at least helps you get the girl. Or the boy. Or from getting your ass kicked.

How to Use This Book

This book was written for aspiring screenwriters, professional screenwriters, students of screenwriting, and screenwriting instructors. Of course, fans of action movies may enjoy it too. The content is the material I find best to teach and in the order I teach it. Below are a few tips specific to wherever you are in your writing journey. Enjoy!

a) *If you're a film student...* read one chapter each week. Read the script recommended and then watch the movie. Then do the writing assignment in line with the topic. Be prepared to discuss the film in class and turn in your weekly assignment for your instructor or classmates to review. Be sure to follow your instructor's recommendations for any variations.

b) *If you're a writing instructor...* assign your students one chapter to read each week. If time permits, ask them to watch the movie recommended. They will benefit from reading the screenplay (or selections from the screenplay) as well. Lectures, twelve in total, should fall in line with the weekly chapters and the semester structure. You may wish to use the chapter subheadings as topics for class discussion and show film clips to illustrate points. I also like to review the homework of one or two students each week in class, so everyone can benefit from instructor feedback. I then partner students in twos so they can all receive feedback and practice the art of collaboration. Please know that nothing here is set in stone. Do what works best for you and your class. While the assignments are structured for students to write pages one to fifty-five of their feature scripts, I often opt to have them write an entire short screenplay (of thirty to forty pages) instead. This allows them the benefit of working on a whole script while supervised and enjoying the satisfaction of finishing a draft they can share with others and submit to competitions. Lastly, while the nature of the material is geared toward writers of the action genre, my hope is that the lessons herein will help writers of all movies.

c) *If you're a screenwriter...* new to the craft or genre, or experienced in the field, know that you've come to the right place. I wrote this book so that it would be approachable, understandable, and beneficial for all. The wonderful thing about writing movies is that anyone can do it. You don't need a crew, a cast, or a camera. You just need this book and something to write on. Read it straight through if you wish. But know it may be beneficial to read a chapter at a time. In between, watch the films I recommend at the end of the chapter. If you have the time, read the scripts first. This will help you see how movies are brought to life from just ink on a page. If you feel you're ready to begin writing, you can get started. The assignments at the end of each chapter will serve as your guide. Get feedback from a friend or family member if you dare. If they write themselves, great. If not, no matter, it will still be helpful. Armed with their feedback, make any changes you feel appropriate and then read another chapter. It will give you the next step toward success. By the end of the book, you will have finished fifty-five pages of your own screenplay and be equipped with the knowledge and drive to finish it.

CHAPTER 1

KILLER CONCEPTS

"A monkey can sell a screenplay," literary agent Bob Hohman once confided. Well, hell. Go sell ours! My writing partner at the time, the talented Chris Parker, and I were broke, shacking up with roommates, typing day and night to make enough money for ramen soup. If it was so easy, why weren't we living high on the hog? We came up with a great idea, or so we thought. While everyone else was looking to the stars to stage an alien invasion, we looked to the ground. What if there were creatures in the core of the earth? Granted, it was a concept that had lingered since the dawn of time, but no one was doing it now. Besides, ours would be different.

We burned the midnight oil, cranking out pages over weeks and months until finally it was ready to send out. That same day the trades announced that Paramount had bought The Core *(Cooper Layne and John Rogers), a screenplay about danger in the center of the planet. Nooooo! All that work for naught. What were we to do? Well, we went to Hennessy's Pub and drank is what we did. And then we thought of a way to turn our idea on its ear. What if our journey to the center of the earth, through the floor of the Aegean Sea, led to the lost city of Atlantis? And there were creatures down*

there! No one was doing that. So we burned more oil and refurbished the draft into Atlantis.

Lo and behold, Bob Hohman sold that to Fox. We didn't make enough money off it to move to Beverly Hills, or even Agoura Hills, but we did make enough to pay our rent in Hermosa Beach for a while. Ecstatic to have sold an idea of our own to a major studio, we went in for meetings raring to rewrite. Whatever they needed, we were game. More action? Done! More suspense? Done! Instead we got... "Can you guys make the characters younger?" Um, what? "Can you make it less scary?" Huh? "Can you make the world more colorful?" Why? "Well, we want this to be an animated children's movie." We returned to the pub.

What's the Big Idea?

Everyone has an idea for a movie. Every waiter in Los Angeles County has a screenplay they're working on. Just tell someone you're reading this book — in Atlanta, in Anchorage, in Instanbul — and they'll tell you they have an idea for a blockbuster. All you have to do is write it, and they'll split the money with you 50/50. Deal, huh? Hardly. As every writer knows, doing the writing *is* the work. Still, the idea is where it all starts. You can be the greatest writer in all the land, but if you're writing a heartwarming character piece about lawn maintenance, it may be a tough sell. Action movies are no different. You can have the biggest explosions, the coolest characters, and the wittiest lines, but if the concept isn't there, an audience won't be either.

Like any relationship, best to start things off on the right foot. What story do you want to tell? What are you going to pour every ounce of your blood, sweat, and tears into for the next six weeks, six months, or six years? Chances are you picked up this book because you have an idea for an action movie. Good. Action movies are hot property. A quick gander at your Fandango or Netflix queue will tell you so. In fact, it is the most revenue-generating genre in the cinema sphere. Your task is coming up with the right one to write. What follows are tips to find it. Be warned, however, that after reading this chapter, you might want to rethink your approach to your idea. Or come up with a new one altogether. That's okay. That's part of the process. And it is far better to start down the right path now than to have to find your way back from the wrong one later.

Where Do Ideas Come From?

Believe it or not, I got my love for action movies from my mom. While most Southern mothers were touting the likes of *Driving Miss Daisy* (Alfred Uhry), my mom was calling me with… "Michael! Did you see that *RoboCop* (Ed Neumeier and Michael Miner)?! My word! When the ED-209 blew that kid away in the meeting?! That was awesommmme!!" Never was there a shortage of ideas that got her excited.

And, in turn, me. But where do all those ideas come from?

Ideas for action movies can come from everywhere. Just look around you. Your job, your dreams, your kids. Within all of them lie nuggets of stories. They just have to be mined. Have you had to fight for custody of your child? Do you toss with nightmares of someone chasing you for a crime you didn't commit? Does your boss make you want to burn down his house? Often the best stories come out of the worst of times.

Consider what you have been through and survived. With health, with work, with relationships. How about those around you? Your friends, your neighbors, your acquaintances. Look at what they are going through. The stories are there if you look. If you listen. If you ask.

History serves as fine fodder for coming up with new stories as well. Are there periods in our nation's evolution that pique your interest? Are there sides to confrontations in faraway lands not yet told? Perhaps some brave characters have gone unacknowledged in the zeitgeist. Legends old and unsung can make fantastic characters as today's heroes. Literally or metaphorically. Sometimes all you have to do is turn them on their ear. Make those knights or queens or wise men and women today's soldiers, presidents, and business titans.

Media is also rife with exciting tales for you to make your own. News, music, magazines, art, books, television, Internet. Surf the whole spectrum for seeds of action inspiration. Just be sure to make them original. Any ideas born of another's creation require you to purchase the rights and give credit where due. Did a horde of chimps break free from the local research lab? Did a band of football players fend off an attacker at their high school? Was a new planet discovered with conditions similar to our own? Just open the newspaper. Your next idea could be there staring back at you.

Imagination is the final frontier. From within can come all. The trick is getting within. Find ways to quiet your mind long enough for ideas to germinate. Meditate. Turn off the radio in the car or the TV in the house. Go for walks alone in the woods. And dare I say it, but you might want to steer clear of caffeine and sugar and Scotch, so there's a clear landing pad for the ideas emerging. Then, as Jungian psychology teaches, ask. And pay attention to what you hear.

Where Will the Ideas Go?

Be sure your idea has the legs to sustain an action film. Many ideas sound great at first blush, but then fizzle out as one-note wonders. Once upon a time, *Saturday Night Live* was actually funny. Even then, those sketches had limitations. They could kill in three minutes. But lasting thirty would be a stretch, let alone 120. Make sure your idea has the potential for enough twists to propel your hero in new directions unforeseen. Examine if it has legitimate grounds for your hero to transform in a realistic way. Look for ways the story will not only engage your audience, but keep them on the edge of their seats until the very end.

Get Fresh

Ideas are a dime a dozen. In the early 1900s, prolific novelist Sir Arthur Quiller-Couch professed there are only seven basic story *plots*:

> ➤ Human vs. Human
> ➤ Human vs. Nature
> ➤ Human vs. God
> ➤ Human vs. Society
> ➤ Human in the Middle
> ➤ Woman and Man
> ➤ Human vs. Himself

According to him and others, all stories fall into one of those seven buckets. This is why it is important for you to make sure that what's in your bucket is different.

If I asked a roomful of people to write an action tale about a ten-year-old boy whose father left when he was a baby and who sets out to find his father when his mother dies, those ten people would tell that story ten different ways, based on each one's own experience, perspective, and imagination. The hero, also known as *protagonist*, could be black or white, the setting city or country, the opponent, also known as *antagonist*, could be mortal or immortal. It's all in the eyes of the scribes.

Lastly, pay attention to the box office. You don't want to go out with a *spec script* (a script written on speculation of sale) that bears a striking resemblance to the *Transformers* sequel (Roberto Orci, Alex Kurtzman, and John Rogers) that landed in theaters last week. Agents look for fresh voices that can tell new stories... regardless of what it may seem like at the theater.

Write What You Know

It's an age-old adage to write what you know. After all, no one is going to know better than you what it feels like to be bitten by a dog, tormented by coworkers, or held up at gunpoint if you've been through it. What if you were a hockey player, an army ranger, or an illegal alien? No matter where you've been or what you've been through, you're going to have a window into experiences few others will.

When it comes to tech talk, cop talk, doc talk, nothing stands out more than writing wrong. Authenticity is paramount no matter your character's culture. Your command of their world will come out in what they say and do. Know how to load an AK-47? Fly an airplane? Sew up a suture? If you have experience and knowledge in a particular space, lean into it.

Expertise will lend credence to your story and get you hired by studio executives as a subject matter expert.

Write What You Want to Know

If this script is going to be your new best friend for a while, why not dive into material you long to learn? Fascinated by the KGB? Passionate about gun rights? Curious about past lives? If so, doing research on your story and characters will be fun. It will also fan the flames of your imagination, bringing forth new ideas in rapid succession. Scenery will appear, conspiracies will emerge, dialogue will speak to you. All because you took the time to look outside of yourself, outside your comfort zone and into the unknown. In the end, you will walk away from the process having learned a few things and grown yourself.

> *If this script is going to be your new best friend for a while, why not dive into material you long to learn?*

Who Cares?

Will anyone actually want to see your movie? Movies are a business. Don't let anyone tell you otherwise. Whether it's an epic for Warner Bros. or an indie for the Poughkeepsie Film Festival, you want people to see it. Movies are expensive. Investors want their money back... and a little extra for their trouble. Besides, what's the point of telling a story if no one wants to watch it? Be aware of who the action moviegoing audience

> *You can't please all the people all the time, so don't try. Just make sure you are entertaining and enlightening the ones you want.*

is, what they're seeing, and what they want to see. However, remember: You can't please all the people all the time, so don't try. Just make sure you are entertaining and enlightening the ones you want.

Got Action?

There are many kinds of movies at the Cineplex: The thriller, comedy, romance, horror, western, sci-fi, and action picture are all popular fare. You have chosen action. Make sure you are clear about your approach to the genre before you begin. Is it action-adventure, action-comedy, action-thriller, action-horror? Whatever you choose, be consistent. Too often movies go off the rails because what began as a lighthearted action-comedy turns into a brooding action-thriller. Be careful experimenting with unproven combos just to be different. A lighthearted, romantic action-tragedy might be a hard sell. Establish the tone of your genre early and maintain it. Is it dry or broad, assertive or aggressive, dark or diabolical? Wavering genres and tones undermine the audience's confidence in the storytelling.

Choose genres and tones you know and love. Action writers will go crazy stuck in soapy melodramas. Heartfelt romance writers will do laps around their kitchen before sitting down to craft a fight scene. Rest assured, it's good to be known in Hollywood for writing a specific genre. If studio executives have an open writing assignment for a buddy-western, they look to their list of ten thousand writers in the *WGA* (Writers Guild of America) and quickly narrow it down to those who demonstrate an aptitude in the space. They're not much for considering writers outside their box. Their jobs are on the line. Your job is to get in the box. And excel there. After you have a few movies produced, then you can try spreading your wings.

Danger Zones

Choosing your *setting* (the time and location of your story) is often as important as choosing the characters within it. First and foremost, you want to make sure it is organic to the story. Is this setting where this story would actually take place? When possible, try to take the audience somewhere they've never been. When *Top Gun* (Jim Cash and Jack Epps Jr.) came out, everyone was excited to be on an aircraft carrier and in the cockpit of F-14s. In *The Bourne Ultimatum* (Tony Gilroy, Scott Z. Burns, George Nolfi, and Robert Ludlum), inside the

life of a CIA operative. In *The Fast and The Furious* (Gary Scott Thompson, Erik Bergquist, and David Ayer), in the world of street racing. Ask yourself where you can take your readers that is interesting. Exciting. Dangerous.

Settings can often be characters unto themselves. The more detail there is to work with, the more fun you can have painting the canvas with the sights and sounds and smells of that locale. For your action sequences, are there practical set pieces to use as obstacles and props to use as weapons? Lastly, be sure that the setting is not only cinematic, but emblematic of your hero's journey, providing ripe scenarios for them to learn their lessons.

Be sure that the setting is not only cinematic, but emblematic of your hero's journey, providing ripe scenarios for them to learn their lessons.

Message in a Bottle

Everyone has something they want to get off their chest. Now's your chance. Our lives are full of moments we can't express ourselves. Let your story be your pulpit. In academic circles, we call this *theme*: the underlying lesson or principle you want to resonate with your audience after they have left the theater. For example:

➤ *Crime doesn't pay.*
➤ *When the going gets tough, the tough get going.*
➤ *Beauty is in the eye of the beholder.*

These ideas may be trite, but are effective. Themes don't have to be cliché to be good. You can make up your own:

➤ *Piracy is the only true form of capitalism.*
➤ *Loving what you do will lead to the one you will love.*
➤ *Losing horribly prepares you to win gracefully.*

Whatever your theme, choose only one. Movies that try to cram too many messages down the throats of their viewers feel congested and confused. In great stories, one strong theme will be reflected in multiple ways by multiple characters. But don't go beating a gong about it. Allow the viewer to pick it up on their own. No one likes to be told how to think. Let alone what to believe.

The best themes require your hero to make a moral choice that bears consequences. Will your hero sacrifice the one he loves to save a hundred strangers? Will an honest cop break the law to keep his partner out of prison? Putting your hero between a rock and a

Putting your hero between a rock and a hard place and forcing them to make a difficult choice is one of the things that connects the character to your audience. We know that place. We face those challenges. And our choices make us who we are.

hard place and forcing them to make a difficult choice is one of the things that connects the character to your audience. We know that place. We face those challenges. And our choices make us who we are.

Roller Coaster Rides

Good action movies are like roller coasters. With ups and downs, twists and turns, fascination and fear. If your story is not raising the pulse, lifting the spirits, and dropping the audience off emotional cliffs, it's not doing its job. Make sure that your initial concept has roots of highs and lows planted firmly in its ground. In memorable films, the audience hides beneath their popcorn with worry, jumps to their feet with victory, and cries on shoulders in defeat. You want viewers to leave the theater exhilarated, drained, and looking at the world differently than when they walked in.

In a meeting at DreamWorks, I once pitched what I believed was the greatest action movie of all time. I touted its strength as having wall-to-wall action. The head of the studio at the time, Jeffrey Katzenberg, politely said, "Well, it can't be." "But it's an action movie!" I exclaimed. He explained you need moments for your characters (and audience) to rest. To reflect on what has transpired and rebuild. If recovery time is minimal, it lessens the significance of the hardship endured. It need not take a lot of screen time, but it should be enough in the character's reality to justify his reentry into battle. If not, he will seem shallow or unaffected for moving forward so quickly after a best friend's death or the sack of a city.

Keep It Simple

Stories have a way of complicating themselves. Once you start unveiling secrets, revealing character, and providing plot twists, the story can take on a life of its own, so start from a simple place. The best stories do. How? Center them on a singular mission of the hero:

➤ Get the gold.

➤ Get the girl.

➤ Get the job.

➤ Get the killer.

➤ Get the trophy.

➤ Get out of jail.

➤ Get off the island.

➤ Get back home.

Once you start unveiling secrets, revealing character, and providing plot twists, the story can take on a life of its own, so start from a simple place.

Get my drift? Any one of these will serve you well and allow even the dimmest of bulbs to follow your story. And that's what you want: a central idea that works for the masses. There can be incredibly clever characters and dialogue and scenes and action all through your story; just keep the core concept something easy to follow.

What Is Your Title?

Pick a title. Yes, now. Yes, it can change. But coming up with a title at the beginning gives you focus. And focus is what you need early. It should reflect the concept and evoke action. Don't try to be too avant-garde. Your title and tagline have to sell the script on a poster or in a guide. The good ones also reflect theme. If you have dual purpose to your title, it will have dual effect. And that's a good thing. Like great stories, great titles are also simple.

DIE HARD

Die Hard (Jeb Stuart and Steven de Souza) is a brilliant action movie that exemplifies many of the elements discussed in this chapter. Sure, it's been

ripped off a hundred times by its own franchise and every other studio in Hollywood, but that's because it works.

> *Die Hard* in the White House (*White House Down* — James Vanderbilt)

> *Die Hard* on Air Force One (*Air Force One* — Andrew W. Marlowe)

> *Die Hard* on a battleship (*Under Siege* — J. F. Lawton)

> *Die Hard* in a bus (*Speed* — Graham Yost)

> *Die Hard* in a phone booth (*Phone Booth* — Larry Cohen)

When *Die Hard* came out, there was nothing quite like it. A hero who

had unresolved issues with his wife had to get her out of a building taken over by thieves. That was it. Once he got her out, guess what happened. Nothing. The movie was over.

Die Hard blew up the box office and was heralded by critics. It's a high-concept idea that can be pitched (and sold) in a line, with a clear desire for your hero (and your audience) to ride from Fade In to Fade Out.

To see this great premise in practice, I recommend you read the script to *Die Hard*. Examine how the writers' telling of the tale is laid out on paper. How the weaving of their words brings the story to life in your mind's eye. Then watch the movie and see how those words were interpreted by an army of cinematic collaborators. Once you have, it will then be time for you to come up with your own concept.

HOMEWORK

READ: *Die Hard*
WATCH: *Die Hard*
WRITE: A one-page concept for your movie

CHAPTER 2

BADASS HEROES

"Hi. I'm Steven." I knew. He was Steven Spielberg. He owned the company that hired me to serve him all hours of the day and night. "Hi. I'm Mike," I said. I was nobody. Just a kid from Georgia with a dream of becoming Steven Spielberg. This was my first big meeting in Hollywood that led to my first big job as his assistant.

"How the hell did you get to work for Steven Spielberg?" I'm often asked. I wasn't related to anyone in the movie business. I didn't sleep with anyone. I didn't have the money to bribe anybody. The answer? I wrote him a letter telling him he was my favorite filmmaker of all time and I would work for him regardless of pay. Of course, I wrote that to ninety-nine other filmmakers too.

New to Los Angeles, I stumbled into the Samuel French Film and Theatre Bookshop on Ventura Boulevard searching for direction. What I found was the Hollywood Creative Directory. *In it someone put the addresses of every top film producer in the city. A firm believer that we make our own fate, I promised myself I would write a hundred letters to everyone I wanted to work for. From Avildsen to Zemeckis. I mailed the letters on a Friday and waited. Weeks went by. Slowly, letters dribbled in. "Thanks, kid. Nothing available. Good luck. Godspeed." I received only one phone call. It was from Amblin Entertainment, Steven Spielberg's company. I met with them. I showered first. I shaved. They hired me.*

After just two weeks at Amblin, I was told Steven's assistant was leaving and asked if I wanted the job. "Is that a trick question?" Turns out it wasn't. Everyone tried to talk me out of it. "It's a no-win situation." "You get blamed for everything." "You have no life," they said.

I started on a Monday. Armed with an assortment of teas and bagels, I found myself on the Columbia Pictures lot doing ADR *(Additional Dialogue Recording) with Steven and Sean Connery on* Indiana Jones and the Last Crusade *(Jeffrey Boam, George*

Lucas, Menno Meyjes, and Phillip Kaufman). The irony is that seeing Raiders of the Lost Ark *(Lawrence Kasdan) in the local theater at Perimeter Mall in Atlanta when I was a kid is what got me wanting to make movies in the first place. I actually recall walking out of the theater that night thinking, "That's what I want to do with my life."*

Over the course of a year, I learned many things working for Steven on Indiana Jones, Always, Arachnophobia, Back to the Future II & III, Joe Versus the Volcano *and* Jurassic Park. *About teas. About bagels. And about characters.*

Bread and Butter

Characters are the bread and butter of every story. With good ones, you can tell tales that will move mankind for all of eternity. Without them, you can't tell nobody nothing. No one will bother to stick around to follow someone they don't care about, that they don't identify with, that they don't long to be or to be with. Ideally, your characters will do all four. There are many different types of characters in stories. But it all starts with the hero. And as they say in *Highlander* (Gregory Widen, Peter Bellwood, and Larry Ferguson), "There can be only one."

The Hero's Journey

The hero is the center of the story. Everything and everyone should revolve around them to serve their journey toward growth. As suggested in Joseph Campbell's monomyth, all characters must face difficult obstacles to evolve. Action heroes must go through absolute hell. After all, a tough gruff cop isn't going to fall into despair and change his ways

> *The hero is the center of the story. Everything and everyone should revolve around them to serve their journey toward growth.*

because he lost his car keys. He must be confronted by overwhelming odds that crush him to a pulp. It is only then that he or she will do things differently. The transformation of the hero is what your story is all about, because it is what we're all about. We're here on this planet for a flash in the pan to learn, grow, evolve. As humans. As parents. As practitioners. Which is why we connect with and root for characters on the same path. To know how your characters will transform, you must first know who they are to begin with.

Who's Your Hero?

The better you know your hero, the easier the writing will be. If you know what makes them tick, the writing will pour out of you. If you don't, it will feel like sludge. If anyone is ever stuck writing, it is most likely because they don't know their hero well enough. Do your homework here and everything else will fall into place. To get to know your hero, ask yourself some questions about them:

- ➤ What do they look like?
- ➤ What is their education?
- ➤ What is their job?
- ➤ What do they eat?
- ➤ What do they wear?
- ➤ Where do they live?
- ➤ What are their fears?
- ➤ What are their quirks?
- ➤ What are their flaws?
- ➤ What are their skills?
- ➤ What are their strengths?
- ➤ What are their weaknesses?
- ➤ What are their dreams?
- ➤ What are their values?
- ➤ Who are their friends?
- ➤ Who are their enemies?
- ➤ What is their family of origin?
- ➤ What is their financial status?
- ➤ What are their religious beliefs?
- ➤ How many lovers have they had?
- ➤ What do they like on their pizza?

These are but a few of the questions you can ask to get to know your hero. There could be hundreds. Not all of the answers will make it into your screenplay, but they will help inform you as the writer. And that knowledge will result in nuances of character coming out that you're not even aware of. No longer will you have to pace about asking yourself what your character would say or do. They just will. Your job will simply be to write it down.

The best way to lay the foundation for your hero is to write a bio on them. Dostoevsky used to write hundreds of pages as background for his characters simply to get his head around them. Granted, he had a bit of an overwriting problem, but his preparation served him well. It will serve you well too. Even if you write a page. It doesn't have to be pretty or poetic. Just write. Unleash a stream of consciousness about your hero:

```
Monty Cumberbund hated dogs. Ever since his
big sister left him alone after school and he
had to fend off a Rottweiler with his Scooby-Doo
lunch box to make it home. Neither of his parents
visited him in the hospital. They were self-
absorbed asswipes. Thirty-two stitches was the
result of the "altercation" and all his parents did
was bitch about the bill. The only one who gave
two shits about Monty was his third-grade teacher,
Miss Abrams. She was kind and sweet and soulful.
And just the kind of woman you want to marry. The
problem was Monty was ten. Far too young for Miss
Abrams. But not her daughter.
```

Action heroes usually have tortured pasts. That's what leads them down their rocky roads in the first place. A nice boy from a nice family in a nice neighborhood doesn't grow up to be a murdering sonuvabitch. Odds are he was locked in his closet as a tyke, beaten by an evil stepfather, or thrown in juvie for a crime he didn't commit. The seeds of his dysfunction are sown early on, providing strong roots for his character to grow... into a cop, agent, or assassin. Some action screenwriters attempt to have Goody-Two-shoes protagonists lead the charge in their

Action heroes usually have tortured pasts. That's what leads them down their rocky roads in the first place.

stories. This may have worked in the old days, but not anymore. Modern-day audiences are too jaded. We want to see broken heroes. And see them get fixed. Why? It gives your characters depth and us hope for being fixed ourselves.

Backstories of action heroes should include training. We like following protagonists who know what they're doing. If a hero is using Tae Kwon Do or an FN F2000 assault rifle or Sikorsky UH-60 Black Hawk helicopter, they better have picked up the know-how somewhere believable. If not, the audience will call "bullshit" and depart the theater.

Desperate heroes make better heroes. Especially in action films. The character who has life by the balls really doesn't need to lay his life on the line. But if the hero has something to lose, they will go to the end of the earth to fulfill their mission.

Want Vs. Need

If by chance you're a skimmer, you know, the kind of reader who blows right past the little words and tries to comprehend the bulk of the content from only the big words, you want to slow down here. If there's nothing else you learn from this book, learn this: There are two things driving all great characters: want and need. Get these right and you're well on your way to writing a great script. Screw these up and there isn't a thing anybody can do to save it.

The *want* is what your hero is after. This is external. Something outside of themselves that is driving them. That they are conscious of. When they obtain it, the story is over. The end.

The *need* is internal. This is the thing happening inside of the hero that is driving them to do what they do. It is most often, if not always, unconscious. It is the broken piece of their psychological fabric that needs repair.

Not until your hero gets what they need should they obtain what they want. For example, they may be selfish. Something made them this way. Their need may stem from something that happened to them recently or, more than likely, something that happened long ago in their past.

In some stories, the hero will achieve their want, but have no need resolved. Those stories feel shallow. On the other hand, many good stories will end with the hero not getting what they want, but getting what they need. Those can still be fulfilling. If neither the want nor need is fulfilled, the audience feels like they wasted two hours of their life.

In action films the "want" must be monumental if the hero is to risk their life to achieve it. And action films are always better if the hero has to risk their life. Along the way, they should have to use every ounce of their strength, skill, and intellect to obtain it. This is what forces them to grow.

Equally important for the action hero is the power of the need. It must be significant enough to justify keeping a strong, skillful, and wise warrior broken. If the biggest hole in their heart is from being dumped on Valentine's Day, it will not justify the challenges the hero has in the present and the audience will not care much to see them heal from it. The best

needs are set up from horrible experiences in the hero's past, which we call *ghosts*.

Haunting Ghosts

We all need therapy. To unpack our baggage from yesteryear. Your characters are no different. They must heal the broken facets of their past to live a healthier life in the present. The *ghost* is the most significant thing haunting them that is driving them to make poor decisions. This is no more evident than in the characters Tom Cruise plays

> *The* ghost *is the most significant thing haunting a character that is driving them to make poor decisions.*

time and again. Usually, his ghost is rooted in a broken and unresolved relationship with his father.

In *Top Gun*, Tom's character, Maverick, is trying to fly better, faster, lower than his father, who was reputed to be a dangerous pilot who cost men lives. His obsessive drive to do so results in the death of his best friend and copilot, Goose. Not until he learns the truth about his father, that he was actually a heroic pilot who sacrificed his own life (and repu-

tation) to save the lives of others, is Tom able to move forward on his own accord in a healthy way. In *A Few Good Men* (Aaron Sorkin), Tom is trying to out-law the memory of his brilliant lawyer father who rose to the high court before passing away. In *Days of Thunder* (Robert Towne), Tom is trying to outrace his dead father, one of the best race car drivers ever. And so on. Great actors choose movies that offer great characters to play. And those characters' personal challenges are often rooted in broken pasts.

Rights and Wrongs

All good characters are right about things and wrong about things. In bad movies, the good guys are always right and the bad guys are always wrong. This feels shallow and empty. Why? Because it's just not real. We're not all black and white. Having characters be right *and* wrong offers them depth, texture, and nuance. For example, a hero's decision to face his foe may be the right one,

All good characters are right about things and wrong about things.

but the reckless route in which he goes about confronting him may jeopardize others. By the same token, an antagonist may have noble intentions, but his method for achieving those goals could be immoral, illegal, or downright dastardly. Characters may also be right regarding business decisions, but wrong about relational ones. Right about policing, but wrong about parenting. Right about weaponry, but wrong about strategy. Their incongruent belief systems will no doubt result in confrontation with the primary antagonist, but will also lead them to collide with others. And these collisions of beliefs are what provide the soil for their growth.

Ethos and Pathos and Logos

The Greeks had it down. Ethos, pathos, and logos are the three primary grounds for which an audience connects with a story's characters. They are:

> ➤ *Ethos — Connecting via trust*
> ➤ *Pathos — Connecting via emotion*
> ➤ *Logos — Connecting via logic*

Establishing trust in a character is the hardest to obtain, but once earned, is difficult to break. If a hero makes a bold choice in the face of adversity, we value his judgment and readily accept his choices going forward. Emotional engagement is the easiest to acquire. Punch someone in the face and you're going to feel sorry for them. Kick them when they're down, and we'll cheer for them to get back up. Logically, we invest in a character's plight when his approach to a situation correlates with our own thinking. If you create situations where your audience connects with your hero via all three — trust, emotion, and logic — the audience will follow your hero anywhere. *Game of Thrones* (David Benioff and D. B. Weiss) does this better than anyone. If you look at how relationships build between characters such as Daenerys and Tyrion, you will see they happen in threes: ethos, pathos, and logos. It's clearly why those characters fall for each other. And why we do too.

Quirky Bastards

No matter what your character has been through (or is going through), it is often their small quirks that remain most memorable. Who doesn't recall Indiana Jones' affinity for his whip or fear of snakes? Strangely, it is often what attracts actors to roles as well. It gives them something to hang their hat (or fedora) on.

Just think of the people you know. Maybe your grandmother sneaks cigs when nobody's watching. Or your coworker binges on bonbons after lunch. Or your brother wears the

same lucky shirt for every game. Everyone has quirks. Bring them to your characters and they will glisten with originality.

One of the biggest action stars of all time is Sylvester Stallone. Some of his most iconic characters had very memorable quirks:

➤ Rocky — bounced a racquetball everywhere he went
➤ Rambo — tied a headband on when going to battle
➤ Cobra — chewed on a matchstick as a nervous tic

Whether your hero spins his gun after he shoots someone, your bad guy blows bubbles with chewing gum, or your love interest is turned on by incense, try to make sure each of your primary characters has a little something that sets them apart from the rest. Not only from one another, but from all the characters in all the movies before them.

Make sure each of your primary characters has a little something that sets them apart from the rest. Not only from one another, but from all the characters in all the movies before them.

Bad Guys

All stories have opponents. Even love stories have foes, which more often than not is the love interest opposite the hero. And, of course, the man, woman, or child standing

in the way of the lovers being together. Action movies require more formidable opponents. The bigger and badder the better. Your hero is only as strong as the beast they defeat. If Luke Skywalker has to take out Bambi with his light saber in *Star Wars* (George Lucas), it's no big deal. He doesn't have to grow much to do it. There is no triumph in the

> *Your hero is only as strong as the beast they defeat.*

victory. Darth Vader, on the other hand, is as big and bad as they come. Defeating him requires Luke to dig down deep, face his darkest demons, and rise to his ultimate potential.

As with your hero, your antagonist should have depth. Few villains think they are evil. They are just pursuing their own wants and operating in dysfunction as a result of their own needs. Some of the best villains are those going to extraordinary lengths to achieve admirable goals. For example, John Travolta in

Swordfish (Skip Woods) or Tommy Lee Jones in *Under Siege* (J. F. Lawton).

Monsters, sharks, dinosaurs, vampires, and aliens can all serve as opponents as well. These otherworldly beasts are easily typified as horrific and relentless, which makes them exceptionally formidable. For they have no rational mind with which to reason. Or do they?

In most great "monster" movies, there is a moment where the hero comes face-to-face with the beast. Where they see the kinship they share and witness the monster's vulnerability. It is in this moment the hero is faced with an all-important moral choice of whether they will become what they have feared — a monster — and kill the beast, or rise to a higher plane of righteousness.

As humans, we are taught to take the high road. It appeals to our rational minds but leaves our vindictive souls unsatisfied. Which is why, in the best stories, the hero makes the right moral choice, but the opponent then makes a dishonorable one, with the last lash of a claw, knife, or bullet, in effort to take the hero down. Couched in a posture of self-defense, the hero is then free to lop off the head of the monster

> *The opponent should face their comeuppance at the hands of the hero, and no one else, or the ending of the movie will be unsatisfying.*

without undermining their own integrity. Ultimately, the opponent should face their comeuppance at the hands of the hero, and no one else, or the ending of the movie will be unsatisfying.

Allied Forces

Allies are your hero's friends. There are many types. The love interest, the best friend, the sidekick, the sage, just to name a few. They are there to support the hero to get them through the tough times. But they are also there to challenge them when they step out of bounds. Fellow soldiers, employees, students, and players can also serve as allies, helping your hero achieve their goal. We revel in the camaraderie between the comrades and scowl at the dissenters.

Action films often have what we term an *opponent-ally*. It is someone you think is your friend, then proves otherwise. This is the double-crosser who undermines all your hero's efforts and results in momentary setbacks in the hero's pursuit of their goal. We usually want to see that person run over by a truck. And in action movies, they often are.

There are also *ally-opponents*. Someone on the other side of the tracks who starts out supporting the antagonist, but who eventually arcs toward the hero's cause, helping them when they least expect it and most need it. It is the minion put upon by their evil boss who proves to have at least one decent bone in their body. The duality of light and dark forces in these smaller characters is what often leads to the most unexpected twists and transformations.

While all supporting characters are in stories to serve the development of the hero, it is important to remember that they are on their own journeys too.

While all supporting characters — secondary, tertiary, or otherwise — are in stories to serve the development of the hero, it is important to remember that they are on their own journeys too. The more they transform themselves, the more powerful and resonant the story will be overall.

Know Thy Hero, Know Thyself

Writing is cathartic. Even if you don't want it to be. How could it not be? You are pouring your heart and soul into your pages, hoping to elicit some kind of emotional response from your reader. And your words come from your experiences. Just the process of putting them on the page, even if no one ever reads them, will be healing. But to share them with others who may learn from them may transform you.

If you are indeed a writer or an artist — someone put on this planet to create — I believe your art is your raison d'être, your reason for being. Some believe we are doomed to make the same mistakes in life unless we learn from them. I believe creatives are destined to make the same mistakes in life unless they write (or sing or paint) about them to help keep others from making those mistakes. So write like it matters.

BRAVEHEART

Braveheart's (Randall Wallace) hero, William Wallace, embodies many of the qualities of the quintessential action hero. We meet him as a boy, young and innocent and naïve to the ways of the world. Then some bad shit happens. The king's ruthless soldiers come from the south and hang his family. He is forced from  his farm and sent away to become a man. Years later he returns to the homeland to reunite with his one and only love. Then her throat is cut. Wallace loses his mind and goes medieval on the king's soldiers in an attempt to avenge her death and bring freedom to his people.

From quasi-birth to grisly death, Wallace travels from the depths of darkness to the highest mountaintops in the name of a cause worth dying for. The film gets a little gratuitous at times, which is easy to have happen when the star is also the director. It's tough to tighten scenes in which you spent hours in the freezing cold, covered in blood, screaming at the top of your lungs. But it is a great film. Say what you will about action star Mel Gibson; may we all be so lucky to make one movie in our lives that offers all the bells and whistles of the iconic hero William Wallace.

HOMEWORK

READ: *Braveheart*

WATCH: *Braveheart*

WRITE: A one-page bio on your hero

CHAPTER 3

TWISTY TURNY PLOTS

It was a Tuesday. We were at Disney. Trying our best to crack the story for Mulan 2. *The first one was a hit. Everyone hoped the second would be too. My writing partner and I were aligned with some of the best and brightest in the animation world. Two directors, two producers, two studio executives. The eight of us were on a mission to break up Mulan and Shang, exploit the popularity of Mushu and Cri-Kee, and get the notorious gang of three married*

off to a trio of princesses in a faraway land. Not a tall order, you would think.

Hours, days, and weeks had passed with us all hammering out the beats of the story until finally we had the building blocks

of the sequel up on color-coded index cards the size of toasters on bulletin boards the size of Buicks in the Frank G. Wells Building on the Disney lot. Given that I was comfortable speaking to a room and often drank too much coffee, I was selected to pitch our approach to the president. I had practiced. I wound up. I laid it out with passion on behalf of the team. Halfway through my groove, she stopped me and gave us all a look. "Guys," she said. "Where is Mulan?" We all did a slow turn to the board. In our effort to get every act popping and every character arcing, we had managed to overlook, well, the star of the movie. She was there. But hidden in the shadows.

Point One: Screwing up structure happens to everyone.

Point Two: Get the story right before you write.

The Three Acts

All stories are broken into three *acts*: a beginning, middle, and an end. That's it. Try to drop one of them and the story falls apart. The beginning is the *introduction* where you introduce everyone and everything you need to set your story in motion. This is Act One. The middle is the *complication* where you complicate everything you already set up. This is Act Two. The end is the *resolution* where you resolve everything you complicated earlier. Act Three. Easy peasy, right? But good act structure is often tossed asunder. For those folks intimidated by the blank page and wondering where to start, start here. The process is much less intimidating this way.

> *All stories are broken into three* acts: *a beginning, middle, and an end. Try to drop one of them and the story falls apart.*

Writing is like hiking a mountain. Standing at the bottom of Mt. Everest looking up at twenty-nine thousand feet of rock, you can't imagine how to make it to the top. But if you do what hikers do and break the climb into stages, it becomes more manageable. Just take it one step at a time.

What's the Point?

The beginning, middle, and end of your story are all separated by what are known as *plot points.* These are major twists that propel your hero from one act to the next, forcing them to make new decisions. The best plot points alter the course of the story in a way neither the hero nor the audience was expecting. Ideally, they drop the hero into a new predicament from which they cannot return. If a hero loses his phone, no big deal, he goes back and finds it. Bad plot point. If a hero loses his job, or his leg, or his virginity, tougher to fix. Good plot point. These unforeseen turns should not only complicate matters for the hero, but also raise the *stakes,* that which is at risk of being gained or lost.

In action films, plot points must be extraordinary. The genre itself implies action and plot points must deliver it. Something must blow up. Someone must get robbed. Somewhere people die. Lies and threats and thefts can all be solid twists in action films, but the good ones literally propel your hero forward. Through the air. Through a wall. Or through time. That is the fix action audiences are accustomed to getting. If they don't get it, they will feel strung out like movie junkies needing a hit.

Do you have to have them? Yeah, you do. Plato, Shakespeare, Hitchcock, Spielberg, Tarantino all have plot points in their work. Because they work. Because we're wanting something to happen. We're wanting progress. You know what they call movies without plot points? *Boring.* If you're sitting in a movie theater and nothing significant happens in the first third of the movie, you're going for Milk Duds and not coming back.

In screenplays, one page is equal to one minute of screen time. So a two-hour movie (120 minutes) is 120 pages. A three-act structure breaks down like this: Plot Point I lands between pages twenty-five and thirty. Plot Point II lands between pages

eighty-five and ninety. But that leaves a dark and murky sea between them of almost sixty pages. In the old days, filmmakers could get away with those few twists. But not today. We're used to getting much more much quicker and need a Midpoint Plot Point around page sixty to bridge the gap. James Cameron says he writes in seven acts. Something that turns your hero's life upside down in an instant and forces them to make a new decision. Regardless of your approach, these essential building blocks turn climbing your mountain of a screenplay into molehills.

The Call to Action

Every action hero is called to action. We meet them set in their dysfunctional ways in their dysfunctional world. Then someone calls. Someone walks in the door. A letter is delivered. With a mission.

> ➤ Indiana Jones, we need you to find an ark.
> (*Raiders of the Lost Ark*)
> ➤ Detective Riggs, we need you to find a killer.
> (*Lethal Weapon* — Shane Black)
> ➤ Ethan Hunt, your mission, should you choose to accept it, find the rabbit's foot. (*Mission: Impossible III* — Alex Kurtzman, Roberto Orci, J. J. Abrams, and Bruce Geller)

This is what's known as the inciting incident of the story and falls around the tenth minute. If you wait much longer, the audience gets antsy. Studio executives do. They have read the books and studied the craft and know where inciting incidents are supposed to go. If they don't find what they're looking for where they're supposed to find it, they toss the script in the trash.

Open or Closed

Is your story *open* or *closed*? These are narrative approaches to consider when crafting mysteries or mysterious elements in a story. It means whether your audience is privy to what the bad guys are doing.

Sometimes your hero knows what the bad guy's up to, but we do not. This leaves us in the dark and impressed by the hero's guile intuiting events to come and beating the opponent at their own game. This is closed.

An open story means we are aware of the bad guy's plans and are rooting for the hero to defeat him, fearing what he might not know is behind the door. If we're both in the dark, we are hungry for information and invested in the hero's pursuit of those answers. If we learn it together, there is an emotional connection in the common *revelation*. If both the audience and the hero are aware of what the bad guys are up to, the film tends to lack luster.

You may choose to alter your approach within a story. For example, your hero may not know who was behind a crime for the first act, but then he figures it out and we, the audience, are trying to catch up. Then we may be brought into the fold for the third act and excited to see the villain brought down. The most important thing to remember is to be clear in your approach.

High Stakes

What is your hero fighting for? For your hero to go to the ends of the earth, face the fire, and risk everything they have in order to get tickets to the opera seems, well, ridiculous. In action films, you want your hero's quest to be worthwhile. Of course, there could be great rewards for their success, but also consider what the consequences of failure may be.

➤ Their fiancé may be killed.
➤ Their daughter could be kidnapped.
➤ Their partner's job could be on the line.
➤ The president could be assassinated.
➤ It could cost them millions of dollars.
➤ They could lose their home.
➤ A bomb may destroy their city.
➤ Secrets may jeopardize their country's security.
➤ Aliens may destroy their world.
➤ They could die.

In all movies, stakes should elevate as the story progresses. But it is imperative in action movies. For example, in the beginning your hero may learn someone has been killed and he is assigned to find the killer. The stakes? If he doesn't find the killer, the crime goes unpunished, the person died in vain, and the killer is free to kill again. That is pretty significant.

In all movies, stakes should elevate as the story progresses. But it is imperative in action movies.

But let's take it a step further. What if the detective's investigation leads him to learn that someone in his department was in on the murder? Now he doesn't know whom he can trust. The integrity of the police force is in question and there's no telling how high the conspiracy goes. Pursuit of the truth now may result in even greater consequences, like the murder of the hero's partner. The hero, in turn, would grow even more determined to find who is behind everything. But this could lead him to uncover his own police chief was in on it. To compound things, the hero's love interest could then be put in danger to keep the hero quiet. Note that in this scenario, not only do the stakes rise, but they also become more personal. His job. His department. His partner. His lover. The more personal,

the better. This is essentially the plot of the classic crime noir film *Witness* (William Kelley, Earl W. Wallace and Pamela Wallace). It is a wonderful script to study to see how to elevate stakes.

Counterattacks

For every step your hero takes in pursuit of their goal, the villain should take a step against them. After all, the villain has their own objective and should be just as, if not more, obsessed with achieving it. In the best action films, the hero's and the opponent's objectives are diametrically opposed. For example, John

> *For every step your hero takes in pursuit of their goal, the villain should take a step against them.*

Malkovich's character's objective in the movie *In the Line of Fire* (Jeff Maguire) is to kill the president. Clint Eastwood's character's objective is to keep the president alive. The more their paths cross, the more opportunity there is for their conflict to grow. Many novice screenwriters have difficulty with this notion, keeping the two characters apart most of the movie hoping simply to build to a satisfying conflict in the climax. But doing so does not exploit the relationship or the characters' growth as significantly as possible.

When the hero and opponent are apart, their branches should still stretch into each other's worlds. If the hero crashes the opponent's safe house, the opponent should blow up the hero's beach house. If the hero kills the opponent's right-hand man, the opponent should kill the hero's brother. The more pain and agony your hero has to endure in order to achieve their goal, the more their mask can be peeled away, forcing them to get to the essence of who they really are. The beauty of this, of course, is the process forces the villain to come to the realization of who they are too.

McGuffins and Red Herrings

When students sign up for screenwriting workshops, they are excited to learn all of the fancy screenwriting terminology. They are then usually bitterly disappointed to learn there is not a lot. In fact, the more we can keep the Hollywood jargon to a minimum and focus on, well, the writing, the better. There are a couple terms, however, everyone jots down to justify sitting in a class.

McGuffin was coined by screenwriter Angus MacPhail, but popularized by famed suspense director Alfred Hitchcock. It is the thing the hero is after. The diamond, the treasure, the gold. This is what your hero is pursuing to achieve their goal.

Red herring is the person or thing that misleads the hero in pursuit of their goal. Coined by polemicist William Cobbett, the red herring is especially important in action films where stories usually require a bit of misdirect, leading your hero down wrong roads.

Rest assured both terms are used readily in story meetings coast to coast and demonstrate a command of the craft. Overuse of them, or any others, however, will have you coming across as a witless wannabe. So tread lightly.

Training Day

There is no easier way to demonstrate a hero's growth than through their training at a particular skill. Show them miss a shooting target at the beginning, struggle through a lot of firing practice, then hit it at the end. *Ta-da.* Transformation. Every fight movie has it in spades. *The Karate Kid* (Robert Mark Kamen), *Rocky* (Sylvester Stallone), *Mulan* (Rita Hsiao, Chris Sanders, Philip LaZebnik, Raymond Singer, and Eugenia Bostwick-Singer). But your hero can train at anything. Knives, swords, guns, tanks, driving, flying, cooking, macramé. It's all in the how.

Rocky was renowned for beating up cow carcasses in the meat locker until his hands and the meat were bloody. The sequence is important as it demonstrates not only the hero's mastering of the sport, but also his devotion and discipline to do so. Nothing comes easy in this world, but those who

There is no easier way to demonstrate a hero's growth than through their training at a particular skill.

are determined make it look easy because they have done the hard work behind the curtain. This can often be done quickly in a montage. And should come at a place in the film just before it is needed.

The Whammo Chart

Today we are constantly being bombarded by multiple stories on multiple screens at the same time. So we must twist and turn at blinding speeds to keep our viewers engaged. The infamous action film producer of *Lethal Weapon, Die Hard,* and *Predator,*

Joel Silver, created what's known as "The Whammo Chart." This requires there be a *whammo* every ten pages in a screenplay. Something we didn't see coming that rocks our world. Somewhere an alarm sounds. Someone pulls out a gun. Something explodes. The action moviegoing audience is primarily males age fourteen to twenty-four, which means their attention spans are, most likely, short. And by all evidence, growing shorter. So keep the whammos coming. Action movies often start on a whammo. They open with someone important getting a bullet in the head. Or their throat slit. Or their car blown up. It's not the inciting incident, but it is usually tied to it. It's the tease that engages the audience and creates the impetus for the hero's call to action.

Juggling Balls

Telling stories is like juggling balls. The balls represent questions raised to which the audience wants answers. Who killed that person? How did they do it? How did they get away? Like all good jugglers, you always want to have a ball or two in the air that keeps your audience following along until the end. Then you want to make sure all your balls have been caught. Except possibly one, if you want to tease the possibility of a sequel. But I wouldn't try to leave any more hanging than that, or your audience will leave the theater feeling deprived.

Hell and Back

In every hero's journey there requires a moment where they think the end has come. They're doomed. They're done for. Truth be known, this is what it takes for most of us to change. This moment of defeat is when all our defenses come tumbling down and we are left to our own devices to extract ourselves from whatever predicament we have landed in. It then takes something remarkable to give us a second chance at life. When contrived, it is referred to by scribes as *deus ex machina*. I call it the *The Spinach*.

The Spinach

In every episode of the old cartoon series *Popeye the Sailor*, the bald and cackly muscleman would be down and out with nowhere to turn until, lo and behold, he would find a can of spinach nearby for him to slurp, chow, or inhale. Invigorated by the strength, energy, and clarity the wonder-vegetable would provide, Popeye would then be ready to rise to new heights to take on his bigger, stronger *archnemesis*, Brutus, to save his one true love, Olive Oyl, from a horrible fate.

In James Bond films, when staring death in the eye, 007 would recall what we had forgotten, that his watch hid a chainsaw, his pen held a gun, or his car could dump explosives. These would all save him from an otherwise inevitable demise. While these remedies may suffice in turning the tide, they often lack the emotional weight with an audience that seeing a hero use their own strength or ingenuity might bring. Regardless of whether the hero's return to power is external or internal, once restored (and in many cases increased), the hero finds himself ready for the final battle.

The Battle

No matter how much your hero confronts his nemesis in the story, there must be an ultimate battle in the third act that decides the final outcome, also known as the *climax*. Formulaic, you say? Try doing an action film without it. You'll fall on your ass. These battles may start any number of ways. With guns, knives, swords, cars, planes, trains, boats, words, but there is no more rewarding resolution to a story than seeing your hero face off with his opponent mano a mano. There is something uncannily raw and real about the eye-to-eye, hand-to-hand combat between the two. Anything less feels like they're phoning it in. Which is why in most action movies, the two combatants are literally stripped of all their devices and left to their simple humanity. Even if your opponent is not human.

> *No matter how much your hero confronts his nemesis in the story, there must be an ultimate battle in the third act that decides the final outcome.*

It's why Steven Spielberg zooms into the eyes of Roy Scheider and the shark in *Jaws* (Peter Benchley and Carl Gottlieb). Or John McTiernan zooms in on

Arnold Schwarzenegger and the alien in *Predator* (Jim Thomas and John Thomas). This is the moment we see the vulnerability in the villain and the hero must decide whether he is to become a killer himself.

The Moral Dilemma

The moral choice. This is what separates us from the animals. From the beasts. From the bad guys. We humans supposedly have a moral compass that directs us, even in our darkest moments, to do the right thing. The question is whether we'll choose to. In good stories, the hero will have to learn his hardest lessons prior to this. In fact, those lessons are what prepares him to make the right choice here. If he is still stuck in a wrongful mindset, he will make the wrong decision (yet again), which will most likely result in his repeating the same dysfunctional cycle of living. If his choice is tangential from his need, it will be somewhat fulfilling, but not completely. If he does make the right choice, he should ultimately get what it is he wanted all along.

The Happy Ending

After the climax comes the *summation*, also called the dénouement. This is where we tie up all the loose ends, resolve everything unresolved, and catch those last balls. You should have established a new *equilibrium*, or status quo, ideally of a higher plane in your hero's life. And most likely, in the lives of those around him. If he went through all of this and no one or nothing changed, it would feel bitterly disappointing. His need should have been remedied, his want should have been fulfilled, and the celebration of it all can now occur. Relationships can be mended and hope can be restored. Your film doesn't have to have a happy ending. But know that audiences tend to like those best. And studios tend to buy more of what audiences like.

> *Your film doesn't have to have a happy ending. But know that audiences tend to like those best. And studios tend to buy more of what audiences like.*

The Outline

I hate to use the word *formula*. *Template* even makes me uneasy. But we all need some place to start. Below is a good one. It's not a mandate. It's merely a jumping-off point. But chances are you'll find most action movies are structured similarly.

PAGE	*STORY POINT*
1–10	Open on a crime/mystery.
	Establish the dysfunctional world.
	Intro the hero and their need.
	Intro the allies and their issues with the hero.
10	The Call to Action introduces the hero's want.
	Intro the opponent and their need.
	Intro the opponent's allies and their problems.
	Hero and opponent clash, complicating hero's job.
	Hero forges new plan to achieve goal.

RAIDERS OF THE LOST ARK

Raiders of the Lost Ark is what started it all for me. It led me to want to be a stuntman. Which led me to want to jump my motor-cross bike off a five-foot wall. Which led me to flip over my handlebars and crack my jaw open on the driveway. Which led me to want to be a writer. Call it a plot point, if you will.

"Wouldn't it be nice to live vicariously through these action heroes?" I thought.

Years later I had the pleasure of meeting Lawrence Kasdan, the esteemed screenwriter of *Raiders of the Lost Ark*. I told him I worked for Steven on *Indiana Jones and the Last Crusade*. He grunted, unimpressed. I told him I went on to write forty screenplays and got eight of them

made. He grunted again. I told him I was now teaching college students to write screenplays. His smile lit up the room and he uttered, "That's great." Again, another turning point for me. Or perhaps validation of an earlier one, that I was on the right path. Strange that Mr. Kasdan was at both junctures for me. But then I imagine he was there for many. A master storyteller with an undeniable wit, he is one of the best ever at structure.

HOMEWORK

READ: *Raiders of the Lost Ark*
WATCH: *Raiders of the Lost Ark*
WRITE: A one-page story outline

CHAPTER 4

LEAN MEAN SCENES

When I left working for Steven, I was gifted a bottle of champagne. I promptly placed it on the shelf beside my computer to open the first time I was paid to write. There it sat. For a while. The spec I was writing was a wise-cracking action tale called Repeat Offender. *It was about an escape artist hired by the government to break a scientist out of a prison in Mexico. The irony is I couldn't get myself out of the script. I wrote in circles for months. My clever triple-crosses left me dizzy and dazed and writing nowhere fast. Mostly because I was consumed by the big picture but had lost sight of the little pictures. Along the way I lost a roommate, a girlfriend, fifteen pounds, and my mind. What I gained was an understanding of how scenes work, and my first option with longtime producer Freddie Fields. It wasn't big money, but it was a start. I popped the champagne overlooking the Pacific with a couple of writing buddies and began my professional writing career.*

What follows in this chapter are the lessons I learned along the way of that script. And every script since. Do yourself a favor. Read these pages. They will help you compose powerful scenes. And keep your girlfriend. Or your boyfriend. Or your marriage.

Little Stories

Great stories are made of great scenes. One after another. Like stories, scenes should have a beginning, middle, and end. There should be one objective in the scene by whichever character is driving it — usually, but not always, the hero. There could be a second objective by the same character, or maybe another. These objectives will either be fulfilled or not. Either way, there will be resolution. When it's resolved, the scene is over.

> *Great stories are made of great scenes. One after another. Like stories, scenes should have a beginning, middle, and end.*

Screenwriter Aaron Sorkin is a master of scene construction. In his brilliant, hour-long television drama *The West Wing*, he would often have a troubled character stride into  the Oval Office in one scene determined to resolve, for example:

1) How to stop terrorists from blowing up an embassy.
2) What to have for lunch.

With extraordinary grace and wit, Sorkin would answer both in about three minutes. There was poetry in his words and rhythm to his narrative, so that upon concluding the scene, he had not only resolved existing questions, but also revealed character and left us at the end of a verbal dance feeling exhilarated.

Push It

There are three ways to create solid scenes. One, make sure every scene is pushing the story forward. If it is not, fix it or lose it. Two, there should be new information imparted to your audience. This essential content is called *exposition*. Three, reveal character. If we learn something new about our hero, or someone else, we remain engaged. Do all three of these things in every scene and your story will be unstoppable.

Crush It

Movies allow us the miracle of compressing time and space. You don't need to be Stephen Hawking to understand this. You do have to be smart enough to use it. Often, beginning screenwriters blabber on incessantly because they feel they have to honor the flow of scenes as they would naturally evolve. But movies are life without the mundane. So find organic ways to move things along. Have a phone ring. Have someone walk in the door. Have a bomb explode if you need, but for God's sake get on with it.

The best way to write around the lowlights is to come into scenes late and get out of them early. If two characters are going to argue over whether to join the army, don't start with them walking into the diner and saying hello, asking how they have been and talking about the weather before they start discussing signing

> *The best way to write around the lowlights is to come into scenes late and get out of them early.*

up. Start the scene with them already there and one of them saying, "You want to what?!" And have the other respond, "Join the army! You should too!" Let the audience catch up. Lay in anything you need afterward. As soon as you have resolved what you need in the scene, get out. There's no need to stick around for them to talk about when and how they're going to join the army. Just cut to their acceptance form being stamped, their bus pulling into the base, or them doing push-ups in basic training.

Fight or Flight

Characters should oppose one another in every scene. If they don't, the scene will fall flat and feel pointless. It doesn't matter if the topic at hand is where to go for dinner or whom to kill first. Conflict breeds drama and drama drives stories. It will fill your scenes

Conflict breeds drama and drama drives stories.

with life and make delivery of exposition natural.

Famed action writer Shane Black does this better than anyone. In *Lethal Weapon, The Last Boy Scout, Last Action Hero, The Long Kiss Goodnight* or *The Nice Guys,* Black plugs two mismatched buddies into setting after setting in which they can't agree on anything. This creates an open field for

hearty discourse without ever forcing dialogue.

Here's an example: Character Bob says, "Let's get sushi for lunch." And character Dave says, "Great." End of scene. No drama. We don't learn anything about anyone or anything. If, however, Bob says, "Let's get sushi for lunch," and Dave says "I hate sushi," then we learn something about Dave, drama ensues, and the scene opens up for conflict:

>   BOB
>   How can you hate sushi?
>
>   DAVE
>   My father was a fisherman and
>   he made me eat raw fish every day.
>
>   BOB
>   Well, how about Italian food?
>
>   DAVE
>   Oh God, no. That's worse!
>
>   BOB
>   Why? Was your mom Italian?
>
>   DAVE
>   No, an Italian man stole my
>   mother from my father.

Conflict makes exposition easy. Or at least easier.

Setups and Payoffs

In stories we revel and rejoice in seeing things set up and paid off. It creates a synergy between author and audience that appeals to our sense of belonging, of being in the know. For example, if someone is trying to quit smoking and they give it up at the end... we are satisfied. If someone always wanted to go to France and they take off for Paris at the end... we are satisfied. This often applies to fulfillment of a character's want or need, but not always. The same thing applies to scenes. So look to set up and pay off scenarios within them too. If your hero is rifling through a kitchen hungry, have them find the Little Debbie Snack Cakes in the last place they expected. If your hero is determined to build an explosive, have them affix the last red wire in the C-4 by the end. The scene will have a sense of structure, completion, and reward.

Space Case

Once I had a student raise his hand in the back of a crowded classroom while I was lecturing. When I called on him, he asked, "Does the writer write the story?" I said yes, that was our responsibility and continued with the lecture. After a few seconds his hand went up again. "Does he have to write what everyone does?" I said yes again, we have to convey the action that takes place in the scenes. Again I lectured. And again his hand went up. Students began to turn. "Does he write what everyone says?" he asked. Yes, we do that as well, I explained. And again his hand went up. Students began to moan. When I called on him this last time, he asked my favorite question of all. "If the writer writes what the story is... and what everyone does... and what everyone says... then what does the director do?" The class burst out laughing. But he made a good point. We don't have to write *everything*. We can leave room in scenes for the reader's own interpretation. You want them engaged, filling in the blanks and bringing their own imagination to the party.

Ticking Clocks

All good action movies have *ticking clocks*. This means there will be dire consequences should an objective not be achieved in a certain amount of time. Sometimes there are actual ticking bombs that will explode if the hero does not deactivate them in time. Other times a cop may be fired if he does not bring in a criminal by the end of the day. These clocks provide a sense of jeopardy and elevate suspense, pulling the audience into the hero's plight.

Scenes can have clocks too. Good ones often do. What happens if the hero does not get the key to the lock before the Doberman returns? What happens if the love interest does not pull the rip cord on her parachute before six thousand feet? Wherever there is pressure, of time and space, the audience will be on the edge of their seat waiting for it to be released.

> *All good action movies have ticking clocks. This means there will be dire consequences should an objective not be achieved in a certain amount of time.*

KILL BILL

Quentin Tarantino is the modern-day master of building suspense in action scenes. He will put two people in a room with a gun... or a knife... or a snake... and just make you suffer. Like Alfred Hitchcock before him, he knows that the

tension lies in milking what *could* happen in the scene more than it actually happening. Many action writers today hurry to the punch. Or the punchline. Instead, take your time.

Paint a picture. Introduce the threat and just leave it there for us to sweat. To see this done with extraordinary skill, watch *Kill Bill: Vol. 1* and *Vol. 2*.

HOMEWORK

READ: *Kill Bill: Vols. 1 and 2*

WATCH: *Kill Bill: Vols. 1 and 2*

WRITE: A four-page story treatment broken down by acts:

> ➤ Page one — Act I
> ➤ Page two — Act II (Part One)
> ➤ Page three — Act II (Part Two)
> ➤ Page four — Act III

CHAPTER 5

FORMAT FUN-KADELIC

I was in college when I wrote my first screenplay. It was an action-comedy called In Security, *about two college grads recruited by the FBI who were set up as fall guys. I wrote it on Microsoft Word. It was a pain in the ass having to tab all over the page to lay it out properly. But it got me an A-. When I got to Los Angeles, I swindled some script format concoction from a floppy disc, then moved to Scriptor, then migrated to Final Draft, which is widely recognized today as the industry standard. I thought I had arrived, that there would be no need for further formatting education. Until my writing partner and I got hired by Disney. They had their own way of doing things. Their own template, in fact, which they required all their writers to use. And*

which threw our formatting all askew.

We had been asked to help with the story for the sequel to Lilo & Stitch, *which had many a scribe before us, and no doubt after. Studios and networks have many cooks in their kitchens and have the challenging task of keeping them all happy. Thus, your best bet is to cook with their ingre-*

*dients. We had to learn the new system and revamp everything we were doing. But here's the thing. Once you're in the system... you're in the system. They like to come back to writers they know. That was one of five animated movies we wrote on for Disney. (*Mulan 2, The Emperor's New Groove 2, 101 Dalmatians 2, and Home on the Range*).*[*] *And it all started with us learning their format.*

> Studios and networks have many cooks in their kitchens and have the challenging task of keeping them all happy. Thus, your best bet is to cook with their ingredients.

---

[*] See appendix for additional credits.

The Big Six

There are six primary elements to formatting a screenplay. Get these down and you can be on your merry way. Different writers and gurus will offer you different ways of formatting. Behold what is below. It works well.

1) *Scene Heading* — Known also as the slug line, the scene heading goes in all caps, flush left, and tells your reader in one line the location and time of day of your scene. The location is preceded by either EXT. for Exterior or INT. for Interior, followed by the locale. This is followed by DAY or NIGHT. Use one space between all breaks in the line. Use an em dash to separate the locale from the time. Keep it all on one line as follows:

```
EXT. OIL REFINERY — DAY
```

2) *Description* — All action in the script goes flush left and is written as you would a paragraph.

```
Towering rusty smokestacks spew black trails of death
into an auburn sky. Winding to a stop between rusty
vats of chemicals rumbles a battered black Humvee.

Out steps a lone mercenary who goes only by TOMAS.
```

3) *Character Heading* — Indicates which character is speaking, the character heading is centered in all caps:

```
                    TOMAS
```

4) *Dialogue* — Centered directly beneath the character heading and indented 2.5 inches on either side is the dialogue each character says:

```
          Where is all this smoke going?
```

5) *Parenthetical* — To be used sparingly is the parenthetical. This is utilized to clarify dialogue meaning, if
necessary, and goes centered in the page between the
character heading and their dialogue.

(peering to the sky)

6) *Transition* — At the end of a scene comes a transition.
It should either be "CUT TO:" or "DISSOLVE TO:"
and be in all caps flush right. These too are often overused. It's best to use them for only significant changes
in time or place.

CUT TO:

Here are a few loose ends:

Start your script with... FADE IN: Flush left in all caps.
End your script with... FADE OUT. Flush right in all caps.
Skip one line between scene heading and action.
Skip one line between action and character headings.
Skip no lines between character headings, parentheticals (if
needed), and dialogue.
Skip one line before and after transitions.

So all together it should look like this:

FADE IN:

EXT. OIL REFINERY — DAY

Towering smokestacks spew black trails of death into
an auburn sky. Winding to a stop between rusty vats
of chemicals rumbles a battered black Humvee.

Out steps a lone mercenary who goes only by TOMAS.

```
                    TOMAS
            (peering to the sky)
        Where is all this smoke going?

                                        CUT TO:
```

Geography

The worst thing you can do to your reader is confuse them. To assure they are clear on what is going on where in a scene, you may want to use what I term *semi-slugs*. These

---

The worst thing you can do to your reader is confuse them.

---

are abbreviated scene headings that go within a scene that let the reader know where they are without all the pomp and circumstance of full scene headings. For example, just a few words can clarify the locale in a house.

```
IN THE KITCHEN

IN THE HALL

AT THE FIREPLACE

AT THE TABLE
```

These short headings flush left in all caps are quick and clean, enabling your reader to remain clear and engaged.

Punctuation 101

Pay attention to the little things. Punctuation, grammar, spelling. If you don't take the time to get these things right writing your script, everyone will wonder why they should take the time to read it. Your job is to give them no reason not to read it. To fall into the pages. And keep turning them until, before they know it, they're at the end wanting to buy it, or produce it, or direct it. How would you feel if you were reading this book and found a typooo in it? Would you feel like the author, the editor, the publisher had let you down? Would you question their profession-alism? Would it undermine your confidence in their ability? Use

Pay attention to the little things. Punctuation, grammar, spelling. If you don't take the time to get these things right writing your script, everyone will wonder why they should take the time to read it.

spell-check. Hire an editor. Ask an obsessive-compulsive friend to give it a read. Do whatever you have to do to get it right.

Get with the Program

Screenwriting software is available to make all of our lives easier. These highly sophisticated computer programs cannot do the writing for you (though some try), but they can lay out the page for you in such an intuitive way that you don't have to think about where you write, just what you write. Just as you once had to learn the "QWERTY" keyboard in typing class, which eventually became second nature, so too will using a screenplay formatting program.

Final Draft is what I recommend if you can afford it. They kindly offer a student and faculty discount. Otherwise, look to spend $250ish for it. If you're just starting out and not sure you want to shell out the big bucks yet, I recommend www. celtx.com. It is an online program that enables writers to work with their template for free. For a while. Then they ask you to sign up as a user. But it's a good place to get your feet wet and handles many of the screenwriting format functions of its pricier siblings.

If you are interested in a lower common denominator, you can use Microsoft Word or Google. Nowadays they both offer simple screenplay formats.

Whatever format you choose, just make sure it works for you and reads professionally. Again, any script not laid out properly is destined for the trash.

For a list of screenwriting software options, see the appendix in the back of this book.

MISSION: IMPOSSIBLE

What would a book about action movies be without *Mission: Impossible?* Tom Cruise was wise to jump on this when he did. And chances are he'll be jumping up and down on it for a while. The franchise offers unlimited potential in storylines and action set pieces. To Cruise's credit, he has long sought to not only produce inno-vative stunts the world has never seen, but to perform them himself. Now that you have been taught the fundamen-tals of formatting, start to think about how you

would lay out one of his scenes in the action movie *Mission: Impossible*. Beginning to end. Then apply that thinking to your own script. What do you see? What do you hear? What do you say? Now it's your turn.

HOMEWORK

READ: *Mission: Impossible*

WATCH: *Mission: Impossible*

WRITE: Pages 1–5 of your script

CHAPTER 6

ACTION!

Action has always been in my blood. Over the years I have been lucky to fire shotguns with Special Forces, shoot semiautomatic weapons with the Secret Service, ride in police chases with the NYPD, pilot private jets, skydive from cargo planes, jump cars, jump off cliffs, snorkel off reefs, rock climb, ice climb, lay down motorcycles, skate half-pipes, raft, canoe, kayak, water-ski, jet-ski, snow-ski and sling stars and nunchakus. I've also been unlucky enough to break my share of bones on football, baseball, and soccer fields.

So it came as no surprise to anyone that my first day on the set of a film I wrote was spent watching a crew of stuntmen run a 100,000 ton freighter into the Long Beach harbor. It was for the arrival of Eddie Murphy's character, Maximillian, in Vampire in Brooklyn.*** *I was like a kid in a candy store. For*

the first time in my life, others were getting a chance to see the kind of action that had been rattling around in my imagination for years.

---

* See appendix for additional credits.

I see a bridge, I see it blowing up. I see a speeding eighteen-wheeler, I see it jackknife. I see a roaring locomotive, I see it derail. Our challenges as action writers are to write these so others see them too.

Painting the Canvas

Movies are cast against an immense white canvas in theaters. Our job is to fill it up. We have to draw images in people's minds so they can envision entire worlds on that screen. This means using sights, sounds, colors, textures, action. Anything we can to bring the stories to life. And we have to do it quickly. In novels, writers have the freedom to go off describing a bar or a boat for pages on end. We get three lines. Then we have to move on. So we have to make our words powerful. Trick one is to choose scenery that is rich and vivid. Trick two is to write it in a way that keeps your reader engaged.

Write Tight

Novelists trying to cross over into the wild and woolly world of screenwriting have a hell of a time. Mostly because they now find themselves confronted with boundaries. There are constraints on page count, act turns, scene design and description. Producers, agents, and executives glaze over seeing chunks of action written in excess of three lines at a time. Perhaps you can push it to four. But nothing more. If your action scene requires more than three or four lines, just skip a line. Then start another chunk of description. It's easier to read that way and breaks up the action organically. You don't need nine lines for a fistfight. Use four. Then four for the foot chase. And four for the shootout. Let those paragraphs be your barometer for moving action forward.

Bullets and Blue Eyes

Directors don't like being told how to direct. So you never have to worry about writing camera direction. PAN, DOLLY, TILT, ZOOM, CLOSE UP, WIDE SHOT, MEDIUM SHOT, LONG SHOT. Toss it all in the hopper. You don't need those terms when reading a Harry Potter book, right? And you see everything in that just fine. Do the same with screenplays. Let your reader get lost in the story. The trick is to write what you want the camera pointed at. For example, if you want us to see a beautiful woman, write that. It will most likely be a wide shot in our mind. But if you want us to see her beautiful blue eyes, write that and we'll be there. If you want us to then see the pouty lips, the soft nape of the neck, the plunging neckline, write those things. In that order. And that's what we will see in our mind's eye. And on screen.

> *Directors don't like being told how to direct.*

It's the same with an action scene. If you want your reader to see a shootout between a cop and a criminal in a hardware store, write what you want the director to shoot. If you write a silver bullet erupts from a black gun, it implies we're tight on the barrel without having to say CLOSE UP or TIGHT ON, which pulls us out of the read. Show us the bullets blow up paint cans one by one, red, yellow, green, and blue, spilling a rainbow of colors onto the tile floor. And that's what we will see.

Act Like a Writer

Just as directors don't like being told how to direct, actors don't like being told how to act. For starters, keep parentheticals to a minimum. They should only be used when essential to clarify direction. For example, if a character walks up to a

crowded bar and wants a drink and
says, "I'll take a beer," to whom
is he talking? The bartender? Or

*Actors don't like being
told how to act.*

the woman beside him? Or the guy beside her? So it may be
helpful to have clarity here with a parenthetical:

```
            GUY
        (to bartender)
    I'll take a beer.
```

Some screenwriters use this space for adverbs, letting us
know *how* the guy orders from the bartender... kindly, boldly,
loudly, coyly, sexily. Again, less is more. Stephen King says you
don't need adverbs at all. Let descriptive verbs do the work.

It's always better to do action in description, if possible.
Still, be mindful of overwriting here as well. If a character is
reluctant to leave the room, you don't have to write:

```
He stops. Turns. Waivers. Stammers. Turns for the
door again. Stops again. Huffs a breath. Gathers his
courage. And finally storms out.
```

Annoying, right? Just tell the actor (and the reader) he is
reluctant to leave. Let them do the math. That is their job.
And I am a firm believer that no one has more insight into
character than actors. They are trained specifically to know the
ins and outs of who they are portraying.

Show, Don't Tell

On the contrary, there's an old saying in screenwriting, "Show,
don't tell." This means you have to describe what you want
us to see. You can't just toss out a broad notion and hope the
reader will get it. For example, if someone writes, "Kelly has
a bad day," what does that mean? What do we see on screen?
You have to write: "Kelly breaks a heel on the curb. Gets water

splashed on her from a passing taxi. Misses her flight by two minutes." Now we know what you're talking about. You're not telling the director how to shoot in these instances. You're telling him what to shoot.

Style and Rhythm

Every writer has their own style. Do you like to write long, prosy sentences giving an air of sophistication to your writing? Do you like writing short, choppy sentences to accelerate the read and build tension? Some writers will use only one- or two-word sentences to really speed things along. Others may even use sound effects to put their reader in the moment, i.e., CRASH! BOOM! BANG! There are countless ways to write. Don't force it. Just do what comes naturally. It will be easier for you. And chances are for the reader, too. Ultimately, your style will allow your voice to stand out from the rest of the writing crowd. Here is an example:

```
Tomas turns the corner and finds…

Five mercenaries in black brandishing guns flashing white.

He dives for cover behind a rusted Buick.
Boom! A shotgun shatters a window.
Bullets riddle the metal doors. Steel wrinkles. Sparks fly.

Tomas draws his Beretta .9mm. Peeks beneath the car, sees…

The feet of all the mercenaries marching toward him.

Bam. Bam. Bam. Bam. Bam.
Five shots. Five ankles. Five mercenaries fall. Writhing.

Now their heads and torsos are in Tomas' sight.
He unloads his clip. The mercs jolt and bleed.
```

Until Tomas' clip is empty.

All is quiet.

Settling dust. Tinkling glass. Moans.

Tomas rises. Brushes the glass from his tux.
And walks away.

Half a page. That's all that took. Clear. Concise. Creative. And plenty of room for the director, stunt coordinator, and actors to interpret the scene how they see fit. Exclamation points can hit diminishing returns after a while, so use those sparingly. Same with ellipses. Drop them in to push the reader to the next line occasionally. But don't get carried away or things will rattle on and on and on....

> *Exclamation points can hit diminishing returns, so use those sparingly.*

Less is more in action films. Don't get caught up in weaving prosy poetic literature. It doesn't lend itself to the genre and it weighs down the read. And frankly, you don't have time in action scripts to do deep dives into the nuances of the Roman architecture you're about to destroy. Keep the action moving. Keep the reader reading.

Build, Build, Build

Like great stories, great action scenes are broken into three sections: a beginning, middle, and end. Of course, they will be bookended by the confrontation that leads to the action and a fulfilling resolution. But even the space between those should have escalation. A car chase that keeps going fast down a dirt road for three minutes doesn't do much for anyone. Throw some cows and fences in there and you're getting somewhere.

Build to a school bus overturning and you're halfway home. Rocket off a bridge across a ravine and smash into a barn sending chickens flying? Done. As Phil Alden Robinson wrote in *Field of*  *Dreams*, "If you build it, they will come." But don't ramble on too long or the audience will get bored. When action starts, plot stops. Not until the action is over and we see who won the fight or got away in the chase does the story resume.

Get Active

Nothing slows your read down more than writing in a passive voice. Drive your sentences forward with strong words and active verbs. Keep everything in the present tense. And avoid "to be" verbs at all costs. Notice below how I replace the "to be" verb with its active equivalent.

```
Jim is walking.
```

```
Jim walks.
```

More active. More powerful. Since our time and space is limited in screenplays, it is best to also be creative in our word choice so it is also more descriptive. Instead of having Jim just "walk," why not write...

```
Jim ambles.
```

```
Jim saunters.
```

Jim stumbles.

Jim rushes.

Jim races.

See the difference? These options
give power not only to the line and
the action, but also to character.
Win, win, win.

*Since our time and space
is limited in screenplays,
it is best to be creative
in our word choice so
it is more descriptive.*

Bombs and Blood

Stunts and special effects are enormous parts of action
movies. In fact, it's hard to make an action movie without
either today. But with film technology advancing as rapidly as
it is, how do you keep up? The good news is you don't have
to worry about it. Very smart, talented, well-paid craftsman
do. Whether it's wires and green-screens or squibs and pyro-
technics, stuntmen, artists and programmers are responsible
for bringing the extraordinary to life. Our job is to come up
with the extraordinary in a way never seen before. But haven't
we seen everything? Maybe *you* have. But how old are you?
Chances are the fourteen-year-old coming in behind you
has not. They weren't
even born when the first
X-Men (Tony DeSanto,
Bryan Singer and David
Hayter) came out. And
there's been seven of
them since then. Still we

have to surprise the action veterans as well. The latest *X-Men*
effort, *Logan* (James Mangold, Scott Frank and Michael
Green), rose to that challenge. We had seen Wolverine slice

and dice for years. But we hadn't seen a young girl do it. We hadn't seen someone with blades in their toes. We hadn't seen new kids with new powers that promise

future audiences new ways to fly and die. How can blades rip open a head differently? How can wild horses and speeding trucks interweave in speeding traffic? How can 2,400 people freeze in a casino while our hero runs between them? This is to say nothing about the science-fiction sequels for such epics as *Avatar* (James Cameron) and *Star Trek* (Roberto Orci and Alex Kurtzman), whose otherworldly action sequences continue to stretch the boundaries of not only creativity, but productivity. It's truly an exciting time to be writing action movies. Because the only limit to what we can put on screen is our imagination.

LETHAL WEAPON

Shane Black has long been the reigning champion of action movie screenwriters. Having sold the original *Lethal Weapon* to Warner Bros. for six figures fresh out of UCLA, Black went on to write or rewrite a slew of action pics that reinvented the

genre. Not only was his action incredibly creative and clever, but the way he wrote inspired a generation of action writers to follow suit. There is energy to his writing. A natural flow that builds

scenes with tension and tempo into a combustible crescendo. But don't take my word for it. See for yourself.

HOMEWORK

READ: *Lethal Weapon*
WATCH: *Lethal Weapon*
WRITE: Pages 6–15 of your script.

CHAPTER 7

SNAPPY DIALOGUE

When I moved back to Atlanta, I was asked to rewrite a movie for Luke Perry, Elaine Hendrix, and LeAnn Rimes called Good Intentions. *It was a small-town comedy set in the South. I jumped at the chance. One, because it was for my good friend, producer Richard Sampson, and two, there is nothing worse than hearing an actor read dialogue not scripted by someone of that world. It makes us Southerners cringe hearing actors rattle on in dialect and vernacular written by those from elsewhere. The original writer, Anthony Stephenson, did a wonderful job crafting a story of comedy and deceit, but it was up to me and the illustrious John Crow to revamp it for the Southern ear. Fortunately, Hendrix and Rimes hailed from the South, so the language rolled off their tongues. We just had to give them the words to work with. But it's not just the words of a world that makes characters resonate with truth. It's their values, their beliefs, their religion. The writers who have spent time in those worlds with those people in real life will write those characters with greater authenticity.*

Crips and Cops

One of the most common mistakes beginning screenwriters make is all their characters sound the same. Why? Because the same person is writing all their dialogue. You. The trick is to distinguish their voices and vocabulary. Crips and cops, rabbis and lifeguards, carpenters and politicians all speak differently. But how do you figure out how? Most people don't hang out with Crips and cops, rabbis and lifeguards. You can read about them. Peruse Wikipedia. Netflix *Baywatch*. But that's only going to get you so far. You're only learning about them through some other writer's lens. If you really want to discover who they are and how they speak, the best thing to do is… buy them a coffee. Visit their work. Dine in their home. And engage. Before you know it, you'll be brimming at the rim with not only their voice, but their beliefs.

Good Values, Bad Manners

There's no quicker way into a character's head than through their mouth. Whatever comes out reveals who they are and what they stand for. Racist, chauvinist, optimist. In fact, if you've done your character work, they may reveal their true identity, their dark and their light, without your even knowing it. That's when writing is at its best.

There's no quicker way into a character's head than through their mouth. Whatever comes out reveals who they are and what they stand for.

The irony is most people don't actually say what they mean. They talk over it. Or under it. Or around it. Fraternity brothers don't say to sorority sisters, "Hello, I'd like to sleep with you." They say "Hi, would you like to get a drink sometime?" A considerate wife won't say, "You're being an asshole" to her condescending husband. She'll say, "Are you sure that's the best idea?" The trick is to not only know what a character would say, but how they would say it.

Nose Biters

Some dialogue some characters would never say. But it is put in screenplays because writers want that information known by the audience. This is called writing *on the nose* and it is a bad, bad thing. It sounds forced and contrived. For example, a boss would never actually say to an underling, "Well, Tim, I would really expect someone who was valedictorian of their senior class, captain of the soccer team, president of the glee club, and volunteer with the Humane Society to hit their winter quarter sales quota." Characters should say what they should say. Not what writers want them to say. If the audience has to catch up, so be it.

> *Characters should say what they should say. Not what writers want them to say. If the audience has to catch up, so be it.*

You want them wondering how, what, where, when, and why. The longing for answers is what keeps them engaged.

Escaping Exposition

How do you escape the evil milieu of exposition when you have information to impart? As mentioned, the best way is through conflict. If two characters disagree, there are plausible grounds for their preferences to come out easily and organically. The second way is through interrogatories. Have people ask questions. "Where are you going?" "When will you be back?" "Who are you going with?" Again, this is a natural way for characters to deliver answers. A third way to divulge information smoothly is by having one character talk about another.

➤ "He's an idiot. He failed eighth grade twice."

➤ "She's brilliant. She was accepted to Berkeley."

➤ "They're going to get divorced. They argue every day."

If you have characters say these things about themselves, it may feel forced. As a general rule in writing, don't force anything. Simply ask yourself... *What would people really say?*

Shut Up

Real writers are compelled to write. Subsequently, they often overwrite. Scenes. Description. Everything. Sometimes bad movies could be made much better by merely cutting down the quantity of what is there. The same goes with dialogue.

Steven Spielberg's first short film that got him noticed by Universal Pictures as a nineteen-year-old filmmaker from Arizona was called *Amblin'*. It was a twenty-minute love story between two sexy teenagers determined to travel across the country to get to the ocean. The storytelling was brilliant. And there was no dialogue at all. It was all done with pictures. So don't be afraid to let the visuals do the work. As with music, the space between the notes is some of the most powerful in a composition.

Hieroglyphics

Yankees. Rednecks. Midwestern farm boys. Accents are plentiful in the U.S. of A. Not to mention overseas. Got a Brit in your film? A cockney bastard from Manchester or an upper crusty from London? How about a French hooker? Or a Latino gent? How do you make their accents sound authentic when writing their dialogue? The good news is you don't have to. Doing so makes it look like hieroglyphics on the page after a while. Consider this:

> BILLY JOE
> You bess git yo' bee-hind down to da
> crick fo' yo mamma finds out ya gawn!

Now imagine that type of dialogue back-to-back in a script from multiple characters. It's enough to make you want to throw the script across the room. (Which incidentally happens often.) Instead, simply say in description or in parenthetical that the character is a redneck and let the reader or, ultimately, the actor do the work. So instead you get this:

> BILLY JOE
> (redneck accent)
> You best get your behind down to
> the creek before your momma finds
> out you're gone!

The words and vernacular are still the same. You're just not having to write the accent. And your readers are not having to decipher your version of hieroglyphics.

Keep It Real

Everybody tries to be cool. Including writers. The irony is you're never cool if you are trying to be. When you try to write cool lines, they fall awkwardly onto the page, splatting in a gruesome cloud of nouns and verbs. Great lines come from great characters

Trying to force lines will lead you off cliffs crafting scenes around dialogue. Let story drive character, and character drive dialogue. The more you keep it real, the more truthful it will feel.

when they're being real. Trying to force lines will lead you off cliffs crafting scenes around dialogue. That's the wrong order. Let story drive character, and character drive dialogue. The more you keep it real, the more truthful it will feel. Famous lines from films are not usually scripted to be that way. They just come out that way:

`"Frankly, my dear, I don't give a damn."`
(*Gone with the Wind* — Margaret Mitchell and Sidney Howard)

`"Here's looking at you, kid."`
(*Casablanca* — Julius Epstein, Phillip Epstein, Howard Koch)

`"I'll be back."`
(*The Terminator* — James Cameron, Gale Ann Hurd, William Wisher)

`"We're going to need a bigger boat."`
(*Jaws* — Peter Benchley and Carl Gottlieb)

`"The fall will probably kill us."`
(*Butch Cassidy and the Sundance Kid* — William Goldman)

"Go ahead. Make my day."

(*Sudden Impact* — Harry Fink, Rita Fink, Joseph Stinson, Earl Smith, Charles Pierce, Dean Riesner)

"Yippee-kiyay, motherfucker."

(*Die Hard* — Jeb Stuart and Steven DeSouza)

BEVERLY HILLS COP

In the 1980s, Eddie Murphy's character in the movie *Beverly Hills Cop* (Daniel Petrie, Jr. and Danilo Bach) was named Axel Foley. Axel had a gift for gab like no other. This was largely in part to the wisecracking craftsmanship of the writers. It was also due to the masterful wordsmithing done by

the talented movie star himself. Discovered as a teenager in the streets and clubs of New York, Murphy had impeccable timing, lightning-speed intellect, and incomparable delivery. As a result, his ability to improvise on *Beverly Hills Cop* and other films always brought classic, unexpected one-liners to the set. The best actors can do this. But they will also be the first to say that it all begins with the script.

HOMEWORK

READ: *Beverly Hills Cop*

WATCH: *Beverly Hills Cop*

WRITE: Pages 16–25 of your script

CHAPTER 8

SNEAKY TRANSITIONS

"How do we get our hero to the beach?" My writing partner and I had a night to get our knight from downtown Los Angeles to Venice Beach in a screenplay titled Swordfight. *The character had traveled through time from medieval France determined to find an elusive magical sword, but we couldn't get him five miles more. The producers were waiting on the script. The studio was waiting on the script. And we had spent all day trying to crack this puzzle. Does he take a bus, a car, a train, a horse, a motorcycle? We went round and round driving ourselves crazy, debating the pros and cons of a thoughtful and practical resolution we agreed upon. Then it hit me. Something my screenwriting professor back at B.U., Dr. John Kelly, had said when I was wrestling with a transition in a short film. "It's a movie! You got your movie magic. Just cut to it. Nobody gives a crap." Sooooo we did. He was right. Nobody batted an eye. We ended one scene with our hero saying "We'll find it!" Then we cut to the sun setting on the beach and him walking into the sand. Problem solved. He was there. Which just goes to show you: Don't sweat semantics. You've got the movie magic.*

Extraction

There are three ways to indicate transitions in screenplays: *cuts*, *dissolves*, and *fades*.

The first is the standard "CUT TO," signifying an immediate transfer of location or time from one scene to the next. Again, CUT TOs are often overused. I recommend only using them when making a significant transition, as in moving from a police precinct lobby to a wharf loading dock. You don't need to use a CUT TO when simply cutting from the police precinct lobby to the police precinct hallway to the police precinct kitchen. You can indicate those shifts in locale by using a scene heading by itself. Such scene heading shortcuts help keep the action flowing. For example:

INT. POLICE PRECINCT — LOBBY — DAY

Captain Jim has had enough of the attitudinal hoodlum.

                    CAPTAIN JIM
                (to his men)
        Get him out of here!

INT. HALLWAY — SAME

Three officers drag the ornery perp out the door.

INT. KITCHEN — LATER

Captain Jim pours Baileys into his and Lt. Fred's coffee.

                    LT. FRED
        Where do you think he'll go?

                    CAPTAIN JIM
        Who cares.

```
                                              CUT TO:

EXT. WHARF — LOADING DOCK — NIGHT

The perp stumbles along the water's edge to a long
black limousine. The door opens and he climbs inside.
```

If you use CUT TOs between every scene, it's easy for readers to lose sight of when you do make real transitions. Some writers choose not to use CUT TOs at all. This also is disorienting, requiring the reader to backtrack to get their bearings after being confused by significant shifts in location or time.

> *If you use CUT TOs between every scene, it's easy for readers to lose sight of when you do make real transitions.*

Many action writers elect to use "SHOCK CUT TO" or "SLAM CUT TO" to indicate it's a quick, hard cut to accentuate a point. But that's overkill. The less you call attention to yourself as the writer in the screenplay, the more your reader can fall into the story.

Another form of transition is "DISSOLVE TO." This is used to indicate a more gradual shift between scenes when one image slowly is *superimposed* over another. Mostly this is used to indicate a passage of time. Be careful not to overuse this or you will hit diminishing returns and the technique will lose its significance when needed.

> *The less you call attention to yourself as the writer in the screenplay, the more your reader can fall into the story.*

Lastly, there is "FADE TO." This simply implies that the scene fades to black. Or white. Or whatever fully colored screen you may desire. This is sometimes used to indicate a major shift in story, such as at a plot point, a death, or a new beginning. Again, use this sparingly.

Cliff-hangers

Great books are heralded as page turners. You never want to put them down because you are anxious to find out what happens next. The same applies to scripts and, more specifically, to scenes. Your job is to create that forward momentum by ending scene after scene in a way that pulls the reader along. There are a few ways to do this. One, go out on a question. The reader then has to go to the next scene to find the answer. For example, you can end one scene with a sheriff asking "Where did the killer go?" Then cut to the killer racing down a back alley. Two, go out on danger. Have someone pull a knife, a gun, a club, or a grenade. We are then eager to see what they are going to do with it. Three, go out on hope, with the potential for

Novice writers end scenes with answers. Expert writers end scenes on questions.

love, sex, wealth, health, or anything else you think serves the story. Novice writers end scenes with answers. Expert writers end scenes on questions.

Hello, Operator

People talk on the phone in movies. But how do you write that in a screenplay? Like this: Introduce one person in a scene as usual. Have him call his girlfriend. CUT TO: Her scene answering the phone. Include a parenthetical that says (into phone) when they both speak. Then simply write: INTERCUT HIM AND HER on a semi-slug line by itself. Then let the dialogue play out as it would as if they were in the same room. If they have action on either side, just write it. Let the reader (or editor) sort it out. This keeps you from having to write scene headings and transitions between all of their dialogue the length of their call. It would look like this:

INT. HANK'S HOUSE — DAY

Hank picks up his phone and dials.

CUT TO:

INT. CAROL'S APARTMENT — DAY

Carol answers her ringing phone.

> CAROL
> (into phone)
> Hello.

INTERCUT HANK AND CAROL

> HANK
> (into phone)
> Hi, Carol? Where the hell
> have you been?

> CAROL
> (into phone)
> Don't talk to me like that,
> you sonuvabitch.

Hank slams his hand on the counter in anger.

> HANK
> (into phone)
> I've been looking for you all
> day!

Carol casually lights a cigarette.

> CAROL
> (into phone)
> I've been busy.

And so on...

Waste of Time

Every screenwriter wants to know how they can flip and flop through time. My advice most often is not to. This befuddles most first-time writers as they had concocted the cleverest of *flashbacks*. Flashbacks are the enemy. Sure, there are exceptions to the rule. Movies with time travel, for instance. (*Memento* – Christopher Nolan and Jonathan Nolan, *Back to the Future* – Robert Zemeckis and Bob Gale, *Arrival* – Eric Heisserer and Ted Chiang). But mostly, starting writers jump on the flashback bandwagon to cheat exposition. And it's just that. A cheat. Don't rely on cutting back in time just to show how your hero was locked in a closet as a kid to justify his fear of being in a closed space in  the present. You should be confident and able enough in your expository abilities to communicate that information in present day without having to pull your reader out of the movie.

If you do feel you must have a flashback, be sure not to cut back to the present the same place you left off. Then there has been no progress. When used well, flashbacks deliver new information that fuels your hero to take new action in the present. Cut back there. To them going to the police, to confronting their father or on the road to get revenge. If you don't push the story forward upon your return, it will feel like it hit a brick wall while you were gone.

Flashing forward is used all the time. We flash forward from scene to scene all day long. Have at it. It's only when you cut from the future back to the present that things can get dicey.

Montages are also a common trick of the trade for covering a great quantity of content expediently. These are far more digestible by audiences as long as they remain chronologically correct. In just a minute of screen time you can jump-cut through five or ten quick clips of a hero training for a mission, preparing for a fight, or getting through flight school. If executed properly, by the end we believe the hero is ready for anything.

Suns and Moons

Visual transitions are one of filmmakers' greatest tools for pushing an audience forward into subsequent scenes. Want to show the passage of night to day? Tilt up from one scene to the moon, dissolve to the sun, and tilt down to a new scene. How about *Highlander*? Where director Russell Mulcahy, in an effort to transition between medieval and modern times, cranes down from a watery battle into the ocean and dissolves to fish swimming in an aquarium in a modern New York City apartment.

Visual transitions are one of filmmakers' greatest tools for pushing an audience forward into subsequent scenes.

Great directors may bring these visual segues to the set upon reading the script, but great writers lay them in too. After all, we have to get readers to turn

pages before a script ever finds its way to production. These cues are also what may get great directors excited about doing the movie in the first place. So be clever, clear, and creative.

THE TERMINATOR

In *The Terminator*, Arnold Schwarzenegger plays an android assassin sent back through time to kill the man who will lead the resistance against the machines trying to take over the earth

in the future. The screenwriters beautifully crafted these transitions in time so that the audience would readily accept this improbable theorem. There are also seamless transitions between Sarah and John Connor trying to evade the relentless pursuit of the Terminator throughout the entire film. The ebbs and flows between future and present, action and reaction, and dream and revelation are done with grace and expedience, always pushing the audience forward from one scene to the next toward a climactic finish.

HOMEWORK

READ: *The Terminator*
WATCH: *The Terminator*
WRITE: Pages 26–35 of your script

CHAPTER 9

PROCESS PROTOCOL

When I started writing in L.A., I had no money for a computer. So I worked on one at Amblin at night after everyone else was gone. It was just me and my imagination. Or so I thought. Until one evening I went to the coffeepot around ten p.m. and noticed the coffee was gone. I traversed the shadowy halls until I found another production assistant working on his own screenplay. Chris Parker and I quickly became friends and read each other's writing. Soon we realized we possessed different strengths as writers, but compatible styles. We swapped ideas to consider partnering on for a while until Chris pitched me Little Outlaws, *a rip-roaring, heartwarming action-adventure for families. It had loads of potential. Now we had to find a new way of writing: together. Would he type? Or would I? Would we work in the same room? Or separate? We found we worked best if we got together to hash out ideas and outlines, then separated for the writing itself. One of us would write the first ten script pages, then hand those off to the other to rewrite them. And so on. We kept doing this until, in the time it took most writers to complete one draft, we had completed two. Soon we optioned the script to Paramount and embarked on a successful eight-year journey writing together.*

No matter if you're writing alone or with someone else, there are a multitude of ways to get the work done. The important thing is just to find what works best for you.

Find the Time

First thing in the morning. Lunch breaks. Weekends. When is the best time to write? Everyone has jobs. Families. Groceries. There's always something. The answer is you *make* the time.

One of the most esteemed writers in Hollywood, Ron Bass, was working full-time as an attorney in Los Angeles when he started writing screenplays. While he was married with young children. So he got up at 4:30 a.m. every day to type before diaper duty. And wrote *Rain Man*. Diablo Cody wrote *Juno* on her lunch breaks. By hand. At the McDonald's. In the Walmart. In Minnesota.

Maybe you're one of the lucky ones who has time to write during the day. But then there's the whole muse thing. The angels. The mojo. The unknown quantity that shows up when you least

expect it. How do you plan for that? Well, if it comes at the same time each day, by all means, lean in to it. Brew yourself up a cup of cocoa at eleven p.m. each night and let her rip.

Be careful, however, of falling into the trap of waiting for inspiration. This is the worst way of procrastinating. Many believe the muse shows up when you do. So pick your favorite desk or couch or watering hole and get on with it. The angels will find you.

Be careful of falling into the trap of waiting for inspiration. This is the worst way of procrastinating.

Whatever you decide, come up with a plan. Work out a schedule. Set some goals. And be consistent. Write one page every night before bed. Or two pages during lunch. Or three pages every weekend. Do whatever you've got to do to move the writing forward. Inevitably, you'll look back at the week or the month or the year happier you wrote something than nothing. And before you know it, you'll find yourself having written those elusive words... "Fade Out."

Hit the Road

Years ago when I was down and out, I sought guidance from a psychic. In a broken-down trailer on a dead-end road in the middle of the California desert, I met a four-hundred-pound blind man who heard from the dead and spoke in tongues. "Never be afraid of running away," he said. "You are a writer. You must go out into the world and fill your well." I never told him I was a writer. I never told him anything. He just knew. He knew there is no better way to find inspiration than

Never be afraid of running away. You are a writer. You must go out into the world and fill your well.

with experience. If you are writing a story and seeking answers, get out of your room, out of your apartment, out of your town. Go out and dig into the world you seek. Immerse yourself in experiences that will drive your imagination. Drive the cars. Ride the horses. Sail the seas. Do anything and everything that will help infuse your writing with creativity and authenticity. Ideas you never considered will come rushing forth. You will learn so much. Not only about others and their world, but you and yours.

Hole in the Page

If you have done your homework building your characters and mapping out your plot, your biggest challenge will probably be getting out of the way. Your characters will talk and act for themselves. We call this phenomenon the "hole in the page." You simply allow the words to come to the screen. From the subconscious mind. Or the imagination. Or the Universe. If you are a spiritual person, this will come more easily to you. If not, it will be harder. There are days I have written five, eight, or even ten pages, finished up happy as a clam, and have no idea what I wrote or where it came from. As any writer will tell you, these are the best days. No need to second-guess what's going on. Just know when you're "in the zone," words come through you. Not from you.

Blood, Sweat, and Tears

I don't like scary movies. Why? Because they're scary. When I'm watching a film, a good film, I'm not on the outside looking in. I am in. I am there. I feel what the characters feel. That's the way it should be. The same goes for when I'm writing. The anxiety a character feels going down a dark alley. The sadness a character feels losing a loved one. The anger a character feels being double-crossed. When you're writing, you should be in it too. It is the best way to capture and convey what you see and hear and feel. Put yourself in those shoes in that space. Get in touch with those emotions. And let them come forth. The more you can open up your heart and soul and spill them onto the page, the easier it will be for the reader to pick them up.

The more you can open up your heart and soul and spill them onto the page, the easier it will be for the reader to pick them up.

Analysis Paralysis

Never let perfection stand in the way of progress. Too often writers will look for reasons in their work not to finish it. They will revise the first act, the first scene, the first line a thousand times to prevent moving forward. Don't do that. Sure, you may want to review the work you did the day before to get your head in the game. Maybe even touch it up a tad. But don't get caught up

Never let perfection stand in the way of progress.

in the past. As mentioned, if you laid out your story properly in the outline phase, you should be headed in the right direction. Get a draft done. Then go back and revise. It will be easier to see the forest from the trees when you can step back and look at it all together at the end.

Enjoy the Ride

They say life is a journey. The same applies to writing. So many writers I know are so focused on finishing the writing they don't enjoy the process. They lament over the task, saying "I don't like writing, I like having written." Want to know my recommendation for them? Don't write. Go camping. Go bake a cake. Go plant a tree. But don't make yourself miserable (and everyone else around you) doing something that can be incredibly fulfilling.

At best, writing is a soulful, meditative, and exciting experience that is to be cherished. If you start looking at it that way, it's not so laborious. Find ways to make it pleasurable. Get some coffee. Put on some music. Light a candle. Want to get out of the house? Find somewhere cool. Inspiring. Pretty. How about an outdoor café, a dark pub, a lakeside park. Writing a race movie? Write at the track. Writing a horse movie? Write at a barn. Frankly, it doesn't matter where you write as long as you do write. When you're done... reward yourself for what you accomplished that day. Eat a Twinkie. Go to a movie. Share the pages with someone you love.

> *It doesn't matter where you write as long as you do write.*

Hooking Up

To partner or not to partner... that is the question posed by many a writer since the dawn of time. There are many perks of having a collaborator to confide in, collaborate with, to count on, but what if they don't like you ending sentences with prepositions? What if they don't like asking rhetorical questions? You're mired in conflict is what. And that's got its slings and arrows too. It's not easy to sleep at night when you're at odds over characters and commas. So ask yourself: Am I invigorated by the process of working with someone else? Inspired to do my best? Able to compromise? If you decide to go down the partnership path, here are a few suggestions:

Find someone compatible in style, so it won't seem like your writing is modern and theirs medieval. But look for a different skill set. If you're a story pro, but need perspective on character growth, find someone who's a champ at that. Select someone who shares the same work ethic, will be candid but tactful in communication, and fills in the blanks when you're staring at the page. Are they willing to go the distance, not only with the writing, but with the selling? Like a marriage, it's not going to be hunky-dory all the time. But in a good partnership, the good times will far outweigh the bad. And in the end, you will have created a kick-ass piece of writing that can win over the blackest of hearts... together.

Writer's Block

Ah, ye olde writer's block. The oft-regaled mental condition that has caused many a writer to drink, caffeinate, and hurt themselves. If Pfizer could come up with a pill for it, I'm sure they would. But they haven't. Thus, we are left to contend with it on our own. Where does it come from? How do we make it go away? Ever stop to think that the drinking and caffeinating we do to contend with the issue might be part of the problem? Not to mention the sugar and Splenda with which we doctor our concoctions? First things first, clear the mind. Eat a vegetable. Do a cleanse. Put down the Diet Coke. Go for a run. Close Facebook. Meditate.

Next, put your ass in the chair. Silly as it may seem, if you don't make time for writing, it isn't going to happen. I don't care how many times you circle the block contemplating an inciting incident. Sit down and face the blank page.

Third, as mentioned earlier, make sure you know where you're going. If you don't know what your hero wants, you'll get stuck in the middle. If you don't know what he needs, you'll get stuck everywhere. Get clear on the answers to those questions and you'll have a fair compass to guide you through most storms.

Lastly, know that not everything is within your power. A difficult pill to swallow, pardon the expression, for writers who think everything they type is. After all, it's just us, a screen, and a keypad. Or is it? If creativity is the spawn of God, then perhaps there's a force greater than us wielding the pen. And it may have its own way of doing things. So don't force it. Instead, listen. The words will come, especially if you're not high on chai.

THELMA & LOUISE

Kallie Khouri wrote *Thelma & Louise* while she was working as a commercial producer in Hollywood. In case you weren't  aware, that's a pretty demanding job. She had put off writing time and time again until she got to a point where she felt she had nothing to lose. Finally, she put pen to paper on her first screenplay and out popped the Academy Award–winning classic starring Susan Sarandon and Geena Davis. A female-driven action story about two women who put things off their whole life until reaching a point they had nothing to lose. How about you? What's keeping you from writing your script?

HOMEWORK

READ: *Thelma & Louise*
WATCH: *Thelma & Louise*
WRITE: Pages 36–45 of your script

CHAPTER 10

PLIGHT OF THE REWRITE

Things don't always go like you plan. Our epic action saga set during the Revolutionary War with Matthew McConaughey attached, called The Traitor, *fell through at Lionsgate. We hadn't sold anything in a while and were at a loss over what to do next. That's when we got the call.*

Mireille Soria at DreamWorks had read our war script and thought we would be a good fit to write an animated movie for

her and Jeffrey Katzenberg called Spirit: Stallion of the Cimarron. *An animated movie? Never crossed our minds. But hey, we were available. They already had a book of a first draft from the highly respected screen-writer John Fusco, but it*

needed a rewrite. We went in and pitched our take. Jeffrey said, "That's nice, but we need a template." He wanted a successful story upon which the foundation of this multimillion-dollar investment could rest. And who could blame him? We combed the Bible, The Iliad, The Odyssey, *the works of Dostoyevsky, and none seemed right. Then I remembered my tenth-grade literature class back at Chamblee High. I pitched* Siddhartha *(Hermann Hesse). We got the job. Together we crafted a new treatment. Once approved, my writing partner and I set off to write the screenplay.*

Over the course of twelve months we worked with the studio launching the project into production, taking it from a staff of six to 160. Our work complete, we left the project. Only to learn they brought Mr. Fusco back at the end to rewrite the narration. He ended up getting sole credit. We got none. This was before the WGA covered animation and screenplay credit was left to the discretion of the studio. We were heartbroken. But we did get paid. To do what many writers dread: rewrite.

Necessary Evil

Hemingway said writing IS rewriting. Of course, that's probably what drove him to drink, but if you know it's part of the deal going in, chances are it will be a smoother ride. The trick is knowing what to look for. Frankly, it's just making sure everything is done that you set out to do. Now's the time to ask yourself hard questions:

> ➤ Is the story clear?
> ➤ Is it interesting?
> ➤ Is my theme resonant?
> ➤ Do my characters arc?
> ➤ Are my scenes scenic?
> ➤ Is my action exciting?
> ➤ Is the story emotional?
> ➤ Is my hero likable?

➤ Are the promises of the action genre being fulfilled?

➤ Do my transitions propel the reader forward?

➤ Have I answered all the questions I raised?

And so on. If you find you have not completed a task to the best of your ability, do it now.

Peeling Onions

Often action writers rush what should take time. Story should be told over the course of the screenplay, not squeezed up front or dumped at the end. See *The Maltese Falcon* (John Huston) or *The Accountant* (Bill Dubuque). Same goes for characters. You don't have to drop everything you know about a character the first time we meet them. You have the whole movie for us to get to know them. Like an onion, make sure those revelations of story or character are peeled back one layer at a time. If you have too much anywhere, now's the time to move it. Remember, your story "ain't broke" until you give it to someone that way, so keep fixing it. Until you have no fixes left.

Like an onion, make sure revelations of story or character are peeled back one layer at a time.

Your story "ain't broke" until you give it to someone that way, so keep fixing it. Until you have no fixes left.

Sex and Violence

MPAA ratings are a thing. Will your action movie get a PG rating? PG-13? R? Action movies can even veer into G and NC-17 lands. But would you want them to? This is an expensive game you're playing. You want your audience to be as broad as possible to maximize financial return.

Beyond the audience, ask yourself what serves the story best. You can be gruesome and violent and sexual if you want to, but do you need to? Do what feels tonally appropriate for the material. Consider what feels right for the character. Many times simply implying the stabbing, the mauling, or the intercourse is enough. Show the blade come down, but not slice the face. Show the lash of the claw, but not the exposed entrails. Show the silhouette of the woman arching her back in the light of the moon, without resorting to porn. There is power in allowing the audience's imagination to fill in the blanks. Simple shifts in language and action can yield millions of dollars of difference.

Am I Pretty?

Too often when writing action we hurry to the draw of the gun or the flip of the car without paying much heed to the sights along the way. We may not get many lines to describe a scene, but our job is to make them count. On first pass, descriptions can be relatively humdrum. When rewriting, have fun livening them up. Instead of...

```
Jack walks into the bar and orders a drink. The
bartender pulls a gun out from beneath the counter.
```

How about...

```
Light sprays into the tavern around Jack's silhouette
in the door. He pushes through the shadows of the seedy
pub to a stool at the end of the bar beside a girl.

He lights a Marlboro. Through the smoky haze he sees…

The barkeep lift an old shotgun from beneath the counter.
```

It's still quick and dirty, but a bit more descriptive. We're feeling the place a bit more now. Do that scene after scene and soon your reader will be feeling the whole movie.

Promises, Promises

You set out to write an action film. So now's the time to ask yourself: Is there enough action? If not, stick some more in there. Make sure it's motivated. Make sure it escalates. Make sure it pushes story forward. If it doesn't, fix it. This is your time to deliver on the promises of the genre. By the same token, if there is a love story, is it romantic? If there's comedy, is it funny? There is nothing more disappointing to an audience than not getting what they came for.

Taking Passes

When you're done with a draft, the notion of rewriting it can be daunting. So it's often best to take it in stages. Don't worry about rewriting the first ten pages or the first act. Just rewrite your hero's dialogue. Make sure they're as witty or brilliant as they should be. To do so, comb through the script and focus on only that. Then call it a day. The next day, focus on

When you're done with a draft, the notion of rewriting it can be daunting. So it's often best to take it in stages.

your villain's dialogue. And so on. Breaking the revisions into passes makes it more manageable.

After the dialogue pass is complete, move on to the descriptions. Are they as visual as they can be? Is the geography clear? Again, don't worry about everything else on this pass. Just focus on descriptions. The next day, look at transitions, making sure they are as smooth as possible. And so on. Before you know it, the whole script will have elevated in quality. One pass at a time.

Last Script Syndrome

Writers of every ilk often suffer from what I term "Last Script Syndrome" or LSS. It is an affliction that compels writers to include everything they can think of in their script for fear it will be the last script they ever write. And it is the downfall of many fine efforts.

Scripts are like stews. You put too much in them, they're not going to taste very good. Beef stock? Great. Tomatoes? Great. Onions, potatoes, paprika? Fantastic. But then some people may think, "Hey, I like chocolate syrup. Why not put chocolate syrup in my stew?" Ugh, right? "Mayonnaise! I love mayonnaise. Why not put that in it?" And so it goes. Too many ingredients equals bad stew. And bad movies. So cook wisely. Once you've done everything you can think of to make your script the best it can be... it's time to cut.

Scripts are like stews. You put too much in them, they're not going to taste very good.

The Chopping Block

There is a good chance some of your favorite lines, beats, or scenes are weakening your story. Print them, frame them, hold a memorial service for them should you like, but if they're not serving the best interest of the script... lose them. How? Toss anything that's not pushing the story forward or revealing character. Lose extraneous dialogue. Eliminate repetition. Tighten descriptions. You might even be able to cut a character. Or two. If you can get away without anything, chances are you never needed it. If you're worried about those moments being lost forever, don't. Just put them on "The Shelf." This is a file I make for every script to house all the lines and scenes I can't bear to lose forever. If you put them there, you know you'll always have them in a safe place. In case you need them for that screenplay one day. Or another one.

Are We There Yet?

When are you finished writing your screenplay? The pros usually write and rewrite and revise up until, well, the last possible second before it's contractually due. When to end is a bit more nebulous for the aspiring writer. You can set yourself goals, but at the end of the day, it's pie in the sky, right? No one is actually waiting for it. I think the best rule of thumb for knowing when you're done is when you start rewriting what you rewrote back to what you originally had written. If you get there, that's it. Step away from the keyboard. That's the best you're going to do. After all, writing is subjective. There is no correct answer. No X = 3.14.

> *The best rule of thumb for knowing when you're done is when you start rewriting what you rewrote back to what you originally had written.*

Just make the script the best it can be for today. Then send it out. And start another.

TOP GUN

Top Gun does many things well. The hero's journey. The tragic love story. The wise sage. The amazing thing about it as the quintessential action movie of the 1980s is that writers Cash and Epps managed to keep us on the edge of our seats even though the hero and the  opponent were never in the same room. They were in different planes, doing dippity-doos around each other in the sky. Missiles and bullets flew by at breakneck speeds. But there was never a face-to-face moment between Tom Cruise and his Russian counterpart. In fact, we barely saw the Russian opponent, save for quick glimpses of him beneath his helmet. The devil was in Tom Cruise himself and in his collision with nearly everyone else around him. His partner. His girlfriend. His superiors. And Iceman. Weaving all that took time. In fact, seven years of rewriting. So take heart. Everyone has to rewrite.

HOMEWORK

READ: *Top Gun*
WATCH: *Top Gun*
WRITE: Pages 46–55 of your script

CHAPTER 11

DEAFENING FEEDBACK

I am not a fan of snakes. I have no problem with mountain lions, grizzly bears, Sasquatches. But snakes? I see a curly stick on the trail and I jump in the lake.

So being offered the opportunity to pitch the sequel to Anaconda *was not high on my list of priorities. Still, my partner and I spent days putting together what we felt was a brilliant, thrilling, emotional story that would take viewers on a wild ride in the swamps and sewers of New Orleans. Then came the big day. We went to pitch our hearts out to the executive at Columbia. Halfway through it, at the peak of our tag team repartee we heard… snoring. That's right. The motherfucker fell asleep. "BAM!" I exclaimed. Just to rattle his ass awake. He just about fell out of his chair. Which I promptly followed by explaining that "a gunshot went off and the snake scrambled back into the sewer."*

We left angry. Defeated. And tired. Endured the lost trek home on the 405 only to find a message awaiting us. We had gotten the green light to pitch our approach to the president of the studio. Go figure. We made a few changes: toned down the humor, elevated the romance, and upped the stakes. Accompanied by the producers, we then went to tell our new and improved slippery tale to head honcho Amy Pascal. We gave the pitch of our lives, but we didn't get the job. Which is just as well. I probably would've had a heart attack on set. Like always, we tried our damnedest. But sometimes the Hollywood winds just don't blow your way. You'll never know though unless you put it out there. And get some feedback.

Throw a Parade

So you finished your script. Hallelujah. Kumbaya. Throw yourself a parade. I mean it. Give yourself a pat on the back. Get a massage. Buy a pet. Do something. Finishing a script, in itself, is a major achievement. Finishing a good one deserves a celebration. There are a lot of us trying to hawk our wares in L.A. and standing out from the fray is difficult. So the least we can do is reward ourselves for our own accomplishment. Finish another script? Throw another parade. Each time you climb a mountain, rejoice in your own personal way. It's good for the soul and the psyche. And you're going to need it to prepare for what comes next.

Be Careful What You Wish For

As the saying goes… "Opinions are like assholes. Everybody's got one." If you ask someone for their opinion of your script, they're going to give it to you. So be careful whom you ask. And how many you ask.

When I first got to Los Angeles, I asked everyone their opinion on my scripts. I was so buried in feedback, it was nearly impossible to dig myself out. Be methodical in the process. Diversify your reading pool so you're getting a cross-section of writers, directors, bakers, and bankers. Young and old, black and white, male and female. I always give a copy to my mom as well. Just so I know at least somebody will think I'm brilliant. Or at least will say so. Look for similarities in the feedback. If different readers are saying your ending feels tonally disjointed from the rest of the story, it's probably worth addressing.

For action films, you certainly want to give your script to people who know the genre. Who see those films. Who will call you out on the banal. And who will applaud you for stretching the boundaries of the norm.

If you ask people to take the time to read your script, you better take the time to listen to them. And be open. In the end, you get to apply whatever you feel is appropriate. Sometimes just a little tweak here and there based on their feedback will make all the difference in the world.

If you ask people to take the time to read your script, you better take the time to listen to them.

Cults and Clubs

Aspiring writers often wonder how they can get feedback on their screenplays. "I don't know anybody," they say. "Google," I say. There are usually writers' groups in your community and many available online. Hop on Facebook and type in "Writers" and chances are a group a stone's throw from your home will pop up. Join them. Join a chat room. Look to universities and writing organizations. You may have to search through the weeds to find action writers, but they're out there. With action being the most popular genre of film, how can they not be? If you're in a town the size of a postage stamp, start your own group and post that. Writers will come out of the woodwork. One way or another, you'll soon be surrounded by like-minded souls filled with similar questions and answers, dreams and desires. Once trust is formed, pages will trade and you will find yourself getting the kind of counsel that will help you make your writing better than ever.

Enter the Dragon

"Should I enter script competitions?" Yes. "But what if someone steals my idea?" Don't worry. People don't just hear an idea and run off and sell it. Still, these are two of the most frequently asked questions in writing workshops. Competitions are a great way to get discovered. Because one of the jobs Hollywood development executives are tasked with is combing contests for fresh meat. Just entering them won't get you much. But winning them will. So will being a finalist. What if you win two contests? Or three? There's no way any exec worth their salt can deny your work a read.

Competitions are a great way to get discovered. Because one of the jobs Hollywood development executives are tasked with is combing contests for fresh meat.

In 2016 Heidi Willis submitted her horror thriller *Black Sunday* to the Atlanta Film Festival's annual screenwriting competition, to which I serve as adviser. From five hundred screenplays sent from all over the world, a panel of readers narrowed it down to the twenty best. They were narrowed to ten. Then to three. Heidi's clearly stood out as the best of the best to me and the others on the awarding committee. A couple months later she drove in from Alabama for the festival to receive adulation from her peers and workshop her script. Before, during, and after the workshop, Heidi learned that, unbeknownst to one another, the Austin, Nashville, Bahamas, and Final Draft competitions had also recognized her script as the best of the best. How? Because it was good! It stood out. And Hollywood came looking for her. All because she had the nerve... to enter the dragon.

The Blacklist

Not the show. Not McCarthy. The Web site. www.blcklst.com

Launched in 2005 by Franklin Leonard, The Black List is the premier runway for unknown writers to take off. You pay a modicum of a fee to get your writing read by everyone who cares to. Every development executive in Hollywood, and perhaps the free world, keeps an eye on it to find the next great writer. According to their Web site in 2017, "Over 225 of its screenplays have been made into feature films. Those films have earned over $19 billion in worldwide box office, have been nominated for 171 Academy Awards, and have won 35, including Best Pictures SLUMDOG MILLIONAIRE (Simon Beaufoy and Vikas Swarup), THE KING'S SPEECH (David Seidler), ARGO (Chris Terrio, Tony Mendez, and Joshua Bearman) and seven of the last twelve screenwriting Oscars." Now more than ever there are ways to get your writing read, reviewed, and recognized. So sign up.

Witch Doctors

Script gurus sit in coffee shops all over Los Angeles, as well as many other cities around the globe. If you're looking to advance your writing game, go to their seminars, their workshops, their classes. No one ever loses by learning too much. You'll find similarities and differences in approach that will eventually lead you to develop your own.

Check out blogs and podcasts of top-rated writers who are in the throes of the business or have escaped to academia. Read John August, Terry Rossio, Doug Richardson, Jen Grisanti. They are all filled with words of wisdom that can help you on your path. Weekly tips from their feeds in social media will also keep you motivated.

If you're looking to advance your writing game, go to seminars, workshops, classes. No one ever loses by learning too much.

You can also contract script doctors to work with you one-on-one. This allows them to focus specifically on your needs. The trick is finding the right one for you and your story. If you want to write an action movie, find a doc who's spent time in that space and knows the twists and turns of the genre. Good ones should be respectful of your time, talent, and dollar. After all, they were once where you are.

Rejecting Rejection

With ideas and opinions coming from every direction, it's easy to be overwhelmed. One of the hardest parts of being a screenwriter is to distance yourself emotionally from the work you had to pour your emotions into. It is certainly not for the weak of heart. Yet sensitive types are often drawn to storytelling. Keep a few things in mind:

> ➤ Everyone's entitled to their opinion.
> ➤ Their opinion may not be right.
> ➤ Their opinion may be right.
> ➤ You get to decide.
> ➤ It's only a movie.

THE BOURNE ULTIMATUM

Jason Bourne is a badass. Lord knows he has to be to endure the bullets and blows thrown his way. No matter where he turns it seems there are  forces trying to complicate his mission and knock him down. The writer's path can feel a bit like this too when getting feedback. There is no shortage of intelligent, creative, driven people telling you what you're doing wrong. Or at least what they would do differently. Just know, that's their job.

How do you weather the storm? If you write a haiku and someone pans it, no big deal. It's three lines. You let it slide off your back. But how do you shake off months of high hopes and hard work? The answer is… you don't have to. Take a page from your hero and cowboy up. Put  on your armor — mental, emotional, physical — and get ready. Just as they're entitled to their opinion, you are entitled to yours.

Be strong. Be resilient. And remember what Tom Hanks' character says in *A League of Their Own* (Lowell Ganz, Babaloo

Mandel, Kim Wilson and Kelly Candaele): "It's not supposed to be easy. If it was easy, everybody would be doing it."

HOMEWORK

READ: *The Bourne Ultimatum*
WATCH: *The Bourne Ultimatum*
WRITE: Revise pages 1–55 of your script

CHAPTER 12

DOWN TO BUSINESS

Hollywood is like an oven. It works on heat. The more people who want your script, the more the market heats up. To get anyone to read your script, you have to create your own heat. But how? Any way you can. Here's what I did to land my first agent and deal.

When you're working for a major studio or production company, you have to sign a document saying they have the first right of refusal on any ideas you come up with while employed there. While many would see this as a drawback, I saw it as an advantage. Here's why: As soon as I finished my original action screenplay, Repeat Offender, *I gave it to my boss at the time, Mike Stenson, then-director of creative affairs at Hollywood Pictures. It was his job to find the next great screenplay and develop it into a movie. He had notes on my script. I did them all, whether I agreed with them or not, because I knew he would be more inclined to support the script if I did. As mandated by Disney law, he then passed it up the ranks at the studio. It wasn't right for them, which I knew because I blew shit up in it and they were Disney. But they thought it might be right for Carolco, the producers of* Rambo *and* The Terminator, *with whom they had a partnership. It was thus released from the studio hold and sent to Carolco. I then sent it to Amblin, the company of my former employer, Steven Spielberg, to give them the chance to bid on it too. While both companies were looking at it, I called all my friends who sat on all the desks as assistants at all the literary agencies I had met while working at the studio and told them Carolco and Amblin were looking at my new spec. My friends told all their bosses this "hot" bit of news and told them I needed an agent. My boss then was kind enough to call the agents to say how much he liked the script and that other agents were looking at it too. The heat was on. By the end of the week, I had signed with the great Bayard Maybank when he was with Triad Artists. The script didn't sell to Carolco or Amblin or anyone for that matter, but it landed me an agent. And with his help, I optioned the script to producer Freddie Fields and netted my first check as a professional screenwriter.*

To Live and Die in L.A.

"Do I have to live in Los Angeles to make it as a screenwriter?" It helps. There. I said it. Not what you wanted to hear? Sorry. If it makes you feel any better, half the screenwriters working in L.A. are asking themselves the same thing. Do I have to live here?

Sure, you can write from anywhere. Your suburban home in Ohio, your beach condo in Destin, your mom's basement in Hackensack. But what do you do then? E-mail it, you say. To whom? If you need an agent, it'll behoove you to be in L.A. to find one. That's where they live, drink, and dine. If you're lucky enough to have an agent already, they can send your script out to producers and studios, but what then? If it sells, you're going to need to be around to develop it with the producers and executives who are a part. Not to mention, everyone else in Hollywood is going to want to meet with you, which is what you want. If it doesn't sell, you can hope that those who read it and like it will want to work with you on another project. Your job is to stoke as many irons in those fires as possible to land a writing assignment. And that takes time. To do that, it's best to be within an hour or two of 90210. And remember, it takes an hour in L.A. to get to the grocery. Once you hit the big time, you might be able to keep a house in the Hamptons, but you're still going to have to make yourself available to the powers that be.

Even in Atlanta, a city that is exploding with film production thanks to the film tax incentive, the productions get their scripts (and paychecks) from Los Angeles. The exception to this rule is, of course, the independent film scribes. They don't have to be anywhere. Except where there's money to finance their films. They may be able to dig it up in their backyard from friends, family, and financiers locally. But more often than not, guess where most indie film money comes from. Los Angeles.

Use Protection

Finally. It's time to get your script out in the world. First things first. Register it with the Writers Guild of America to protect the rights. You can do it here: https://www.wgawregistry.org

Trust me, trust them. They've been protecting ideas just like yours since 1927. It takes three minutes. Costs twenty bucks. And anyone can do it. Simply click on the link, fill out the form with your name, address, title of the project, logline, and date of submission. Enter your credit card number, upload the screenplay, and voila, you are protected. Should you copyright it, patent it, mail a certified copy

Register your script with the Writers Guild of America to protect the rights.

to yourself? No need. Once you register it with the guild, it's stored for five years. If after five years you haven't been able to do anything with the idea and you're still afraid of it getting stolen, you can re-register it.

How Do I Get an Agent?

"How do I get an agent?" is probably the most commonly asked question by aspiring screenwriters. After all, you can't get work as a screenwriter without an agent, but no agent wants to represent you unless you have work. So how do you do it? Once your script is registered, send it to anyone who knows anyone who has a connection to agents in Hollywood. It could be your aunt Martha's dentist in Minneapolis who has a son-in-law who is sleeping with a girl whose roommate is an assistant to Mila Kunis. People aren't crazy about being asked to help but do like being asked for advice. So politely ask if they have the time to tell you what they think of your script. If they think it's good, ask if there's someone they know at an agency who might like to read it. Chances are they do. Thank them profusely for sending it over and start the process again. It's best to find an agent, or agent's assistant, who's young and hungry and looking for the next big thing. And there are plenty of them out there. They get 10% of everything you make. Follow up with them, but don't stalk them. They have hundreds of scripts to read and are doing their best just to keep their heads above water. If your script is great, you should get a call. Their job is to find you.

Do I Need a Manager?

You do not need a manager. But it sure as hell helps. The more people you have on your side hawking your wares and singing your praises, the better. After all, your agent can only do so many lunches in a week. Managers' duties tend to be more personal, more attentive, more often. They have fewer clients, generally, and thus can devote more time to help guide you on your career path.

> *You do not need a manager. But it sure as hell helps.*

Which projects do you take? Which meetings do you attend? Who else should you get to know? They are really in the relationship business. The catch is, they usually take 15% of your bottom line. That's not chump change. But remember, if they get you more jobs, there's more money to go around.

Why Do I Need an Attorney?

"If I have an agent and/or a manager, why do I need an attorney?" Because they do different things. Agents and managers get your writing read, get you considered for jobs, get you in the room with the buyers, and agents negotiate the top lines of the deal. Beneath those top lines are a lot of other lines. Sometimes twenty pages' worth of fine print. For merchandising rights in Norway. Home video residuals in Uganda. And airline revenues at thirty thousand feet. No agents have time for that. They're out beating the bushes for the next gig for you or another client. That's where attorneys come in. They have stacks of precedents they can draw from to assure that you are getting your just due on the details of the deal. And that makes them worth every penny of their 5% take.

How Do I Get in the WGA?

The Writers Guild of America is the union that represents all screenwriters. It is broken into two components, the East Coast (WGAE) and West Coast (WGAW). Most screenwriters are represented by the West Coast, for that's where most screenwriting deals go down. The East Coast has their hand in the pot, but they tend to represent writers of content that originates in New York and Washington, such as news, soaps, and reality.

Getting in the WGA is also a Catch-22. You can't get in without being hired for a project covered by one of their signatories and you can't get hired by one of their signatories without a project. The trick is to get someone who is operating as a signatory to want to buy your script or hire you to write one. Then you will be sent a letter from the WGA welcoming you to the organization. It goes something like this:

"Congratulations! Your screenplay has been bought by Warner Bros. for a gazillion dollars. They are a signatory of the WGA. So you must join us. To do so, please send us $3,000 dollars within the next thirty days. Once you join, we will take 1½% of everything you make as a writer for the rest of your life. Have a nice day."

The funny thing is... you want that letter. The WGA is a godsend. They provide some of the best medical benefits in the country. A pension plan. Guaranteed pay minimums. Arbitration processes. And legal protection. They defend their writers at every turn. Dues paid them are a drop in the bucket from what you are able to receive in working on projects within their jurisdiction.

If you're not writing in Hollywood, guild membership may not behoove you. Why? Because there are plenty of non-guild producers and studios developing independent content for alternative distribution. Producers may not have the guild minimum of $49,000 for a low-budget feature screenplay, but they might have $20,000. Would you be willing to write a movie for that? Or perhaps it's a small animated upstart wanting you to write three-minute webisodes for $1,000 a pop. Point being, the world is changing. If you're in the big leagues in Hollywood, you want to be in the WGA. But if you're in Peoria, it may not pay to be. You decide.

If you're not writing in Hollywood, guild membership may not behoove you.

Cover Me

Somehow someway you figured out how to get your script to someone somewhere. An agent, actor, producer, director, or studio executive. Now you sit on pins and needles awaiting their feedback. News flash: They're not going to read it. They never do. At first. *Readers* do.

Readers are the first wave of defense at production companies and studios. Executives are so swamped with all the scripts they receive every month, they only have time to read the best. So they have *readers* read them first. Readers are smart, talented writers and development personnel trained to evaluate your screenplay. They have been schooled in the doctrines herein as well as the whims and ways for whomever they're reading. They know exactly what to look for and are charged with encapsulating your 120 pages of months of work into a two-page review called *coverage*.

Coverage is usually broken into two pages. The first page starts with essential information regarding submission. Who sent what by whom to whom via whom when:

CRASH! BOOM! BANG!

MICHAEL LUCKER

TITLE:	Awesome Screenplay	DATE:	July 10, 2017
WRITTEN BY:	Molly Screenwriter	ANALYST:	Joe Readsalot
GENRE:	Action	SUBMITTED BY:	Agent Dan
FORMAT:	Screenplay/119 pgs	SUBMITTED TO:	VP Marcy

Next is the logline, which gives the essence of the story in one or two lines.

LOGLINE: When a lowly screenwriter's script is rejected by Hollywood, he sets out to burn down all of the studios. Captured and imprisoned, his life story is turned into an Academy Award—winning movie written by someone else.

After that comes an objective telling of the story, which uses the rest of the first page. Good readers break this into three paragraphs representing the three acts, which enables busy development executives to review and digest the material swiftly.

At the bottom of the page comes "the box." This allows the reader to articulate very succinctly the strengths and weaknesses of the screenplay. At the bottom of the box lies a recommendation panel where the reader indicates one of three options: RECOMMEND, CONSIDER, or PASS.

	Excellent	Good	Fair	Poor
Concept	X			
Character			X	
Plot		X		
Dialogue		X		
Pacing			X	
Recommendation	CONSIDER			

Page two of the coverage is where the reader gives their *subjective* opinion of the material called COMMENTS. These can be scathing. They can also be complimentary. Here the reader offers in-depth analysis of the script and the writer's strengths and weaknesses. Great readers offer suggestions for remedying the challenges. It's important they always be candid. Their jobs and the jobs of the execs to whom they are providing the coverage are on the line.

If you're looking to break into the creative side of the entertainment industry, working as a reader is a great place to start. You're reading lots of material, learning what the studios are looking for, and forging relationships that may last a lifetime.

Devo Girls

The next wave of defense at the studio are the *Devo Girls*. Short for "Development." Not meant to be derogatory, but often taken that way. They're not always women, but they usually are. They're not always well educated, but they usually are. They're not always attractive, but they usually are. They are the right hands of the kings or the queens of the studios or production companies. Their job is to develop professional relationships with writers and directors and agents and identify and foster the next big project. They're the ones who generally review all the coverage and decide what will be handed up the ranks to superiors. They actually read the scripts the readers recommend. Often ten a week. So be nice to them. They are overworked and underpaid. They grow up to be screenwriters, producers, and studio presidents.

Many action writers are men. Macho men at that, who might make the mistake of writing female characters with the depth of petri dishes. I would encourage you not to. Weak women make weak characters and weak characters make weak screenplays. In addition, you will find that the very smart, soulful, and opinionated women reading your screenplay in development would just as soon paper the walls of the bathroom with a condescending script than pass it up the ranks.

Pride and Prejudice

When I teamed up with my writing partner, one of the first things we did together was hang a sign above our office entrance that read: PLEASE CHECK YOUR EGO AT THE DOOR. It was a constant reminder to leave our personal pride and prejudices outside the room when writing. "Let the script take precedence," we would say. The challenge, of course, is that we, or you, or anyone, may differ on what is best for the script. This holds especially true when receiving feedback from development executives you may be working with. They're entitled to their opinions. And their short time with you in the room may be their only opportunity to impress upon you what they hope you do with the script before you leave. Remember they wouldn't be meeting with you if they didn't like the script in the first place. So listen up.

Sold!

Today is the day. Some studio wants to buy your screenplay. What do you do? Well, nothing, actually. Your job is to sit by the phone and not have a nervous breakdown. Your agent, on the other hand, is going to be busy. When the studio makes an offer, your agent will buy some time to let every other studio in town know. The idea, of course, is to heat up the market and create an auction over your "hot" action script. The studios have been down this road before, so will try to limit the time the agent has to ascertain an answer from you. The dance will go on until your agent thinks they got you the best offer they can based on competitive offers, WGA minimums, industry standard, and your going rate, if any. Then they call you and present you the offer. It is up to you to accept it or not.

Guild minimum for a high-budget feature as of this writing (2017) is $127,295. Sound good? Want to take it? Consider this: Uncle Sam gets 33 1/3%. The agent gets 10%. The attorney gets 5%. The WGA gets 1½%. Now you're down to about $63,000. If you have a manager, they would take 15%. If you have a partner, they would take 50%. Still want to take it? Your agent can go to bat for more. Just know that if they do, the studio may withdraw the offer. Eek!

Development Hell

Hurray! Your script is now owned by the studio. *Now what?* Well, now it gets developed. *Why?* No movies are automatically greenlit for production. *Why?* They need actors and directors and producers attached. And nine times out of ten the studio feels the scripts need work before they are sent to those people to consider. It could be any number of things. Perhaps the characters need fleshing out, the end needs to be amped up, or the budget cut down. Or the studio executives simply feel the need to put in their two cents.

Welcome to development, the land of misfit scripts. At any one time a studio may have up to a hundred scripts in development that they are trying to rewrite and *package*. Some may be original screenplays bought off the street. Others may be books or articles they have the rights to. Each time someone new is brought onto the project they get to put in their two cents. Which means the script needs to be rewritten. If your agent did a good job negotiating and/or you are protected under the provinces of the guild, you will get

At any one time a studio may have up to a hundred scripts in development that they are trying to rewrite and package.

first crack. If you do well, you will get second crack. There could be many cracks. It depends on how well you do and how long the project takes to develop. Deciding whether the project is ready for production is the discretion of the studio president.

Deciding whether the project is ready for production is the discretion of the studio president.

Rent Control

If your script did not sell, don't lose heart. Unless you went and bought a boat. Then you can lose your mind. Never put the cart before the horse. But just because a studio wasn't ready to pony up six figures for your pages doesn't mean they don't want it. They might be willing to option it.

Optioning a script means they are renting the rights for a certain amount of time, usually six to twelve months. These fees are nominal, subject to industry standard and norms, and are usually in the $2,000 to $10,000 range. Optioning allows them to test the waters without delving deep into their development fund. During this time the studio, or in some cases producers, will try to attach elements to move the project forward. The good news is that option agreements almost always include the purchase price, so you are already in line for more money should your project get off the ground.

Hired Guns

Let's say no one wanted your script. Don't shop for razor blades just yet. Perhaps someone who read it liked the writing enough to hire you to write another project. Agents send out scripts all the time for just this reason, to serve as *writing samples.* Maybe you wrote an action-thriller set in a nuclear missile silo. They didn't want that, but they thought you did a good job weaving tense and terse dialogue in the heat of the moment and think you would do a good job writing (or rewriting) their action thriller set in a space station. They will call your agent and make you an offer. Some writers have no interest in rewriting other's screenplays. We call those writers *rich.* Most writers, in the dog-eat-dog world of moviemaking, are thrilled to have the opportunity to write on anything they believe in. And that's the key. Just as you should believe in the script you were writing on spec, so too should you believe in the one handed to you to rewrite. If not, it will show through.

The Windup, The Pitch

If no one bought your script, optioned your script, or hired you to write a script, still there is hope. Maybe that writing sample convinced the studios that you are an action genius and may write the next blockbuster. But what is it? Now's your chance to pitch them a new idea. Come up with your best one and get ready. Have that concept worked out so

> *If no one bought your script, optioned your script, or hired you to write a script, still there is hope.*

well in your head that you don't need notes. You want to be able to look them straight in the eye and convince them the idea is brilliant.

You usually get twenty minutes to pitch, give or take. You don't have to pitch every detail. In fact, leaving room for their imagination is good. Start with something that will get them thinking. Something that teases the idea and the theme. I think asking a question works best, such as:

> Do you believe in ghosts?
> Have you ever been to Africa?
> Has anyone in your family served in the military?

Follow it up with a line or two that pays off the question and teases the story. Then get into it with efficiency and passion. There are a lot of different things different writers say to include in a pitch. I think you should include these:

PITCH BITS:

> *The tease*
> *The open*
> *The hero's need*
> *The inciting incident*
> *The hero's want*
> *The opponent's want*
> *The first act turn*
> *The midpoint turn*
> *A great action scene*
> *The second act turn*
> *The theme*
> *The end*

Some writers think you should hold back the ending, leaving the execs having to pay to hear it. You know what we call those writers? *Unemployed.* This is the room where you tell the end. Just have it be a great ending that makes them want to see the movie. If they have questions, good. Let them ask. If they have suggestions, even better. Once they are involved in the creative process and taking ownership of the idea, they will be more invested in seeing your (and "their") idea succeed.

Don't lose sleep over pitches. You want to do well in the room, yes, but pitches are hard to sell. You think selling a script is tough? Few studios will take the chance on buying something that's not even written yet. Win, lose, or draw in the room, you're developing your relationship with the execs and giving them an idea of the kind of stories you are excited to tell.

Pay the Piper

"How do I get paid?" It works like this: If you sell a script, your payment will be broken into installments, usually five. You get paid for the script (and rights) up front. The remainder is paid for services rendered on rewrites. For example, if you sell your script to Paramount for $150,000, they may pay you $100,000 upon close of the deal, then break rewrites into two phases: the first at $30,000, the second at $20,000. Each time you commence writing you get paid half of the amount due. You get the other half upon completion. Here's an example:

PURCHASE PRICE	$150,000
FIRST PAYMENT	$100,000
COMMENCE FIRST REWRITE	$15,000
COMPLETE FIRST REWRITE	$15,000
COMMENCE SECOND REWRITE	$10,000
COMPLETE SECOND REWRITE	$10,000

You are also subject to receive production bonuses, which are negotiable subject to WGA minimums. This means that if the movie actually gets made, you receive more money. This is usually more than the purchase price. This money no longer comes out of the studio's development fund, but out

of the production budget for the movie itself. If you received $150,000 for the draft and two sets of revisions, you may get $300,000 as a bonus for the movie getting made. This too is broken into halves, paid 50% upon commencement of principal photography and 50% upon completion. All payments must be made on contractual timelines, usually within thirty or sixty days. Bonus payments are often referred to in deals as "against" sums. So your take on your script sale if the movie gets made would be $150,000 against $450,000.

Residuals are paid after the movie is released. The WGA tracks this revenue through studio accounting departments and returns to you your share. These fees are traditionally around 2½% net profit per WGA minimums and increased based on your success as a writer. The biggest payments are usually paid out as a result of the largest amount of revenue generated from theatrical box office release. Checks are sent to you quarterly from the WGA. After the movie has left the theaters and those sums have been paid, you should still see some money coming in from ancillary distribution avenues such as network, cable, video, and streaming, as well as merchandising or any other rights included in the deal. If you wrote a successful movie, these checks may come for a long, long time.

Why Not You?

So your script didn't sell. So what? Write another one. So your script sold. So what? Write another one. Writers write. Every day, time permitting. Writing is in their blood. And if you made it this far in the book, chances are it's in your blood too.

There are thousands of "wannabe" writers with lots of ideas. But how many of them actually study the craft? How many actually do the work? How many actually send out their scripts? Apply the lessons herein and I assure you that you will be ahead of the pack. Put your heart and soul into it. Tell a tale you feel must be told. And late at night when you're all alone with your tea and your candle and your laptop and voices are saying that it can't be done, you'll never make it, it's too hard, just remember:

Someone has to write movies. Why not you?

THE MATRIX

I can think of no better movie to illustrate the nature of the movie business than *The Matrix* (the Wachowskis). An intricate web of truths and lies operating in multiple spheres of reality, the world is filled with simple mortals trying haplessly to decipher the puzzle of life and win the war against the drones.

When the Wachowskis first introduced the concept to the world, it was a mind-blowing experiment in complex layers of consciousness. What is real? What is not? So too is the movie business. It is, after all, a business of make-believe. You just have to make it work for you, by hook or by crook, hard work or soft sell, motivation or manifestation, paying your dues or praying to heaven. Now's your chance.

HOMEWORK

READ: *The Matrix*

WATCH: *The Matrix*

WRITE: Pages 56–110. You're halfway there!

GRATITUDE

I have been lucky to have great writing teachers like Dr. John Kelly at Boston University's College of Communication, and Professor Bill Lawson who taught me how to think visually. Before them there were Ms. McMillan, Ms. Ondilla, Ms. Powell, Ms. Perry, Ms. Bubenheim. All gifted educators from my youth who made learning fun. And inspired me to do the same for others. I also had great friends like Bret, Jimmy, and Tony, who not only would take a bullet for me in high school, but spent mornings before the bell showing me the difference between an adverb and a hole in the ground.

In Los Angeles I have had the pleasure of working with some of the brightest minds in the film industry: Steven Spielberg, Kathleen Kennedy, Deb Newmeyer, Jeffrey Katzenberg, Mike Stenson, Chip Diggins, John Baldecchi, Stephen Sommers, Andy Fickman, Wes Craven, Marianne Maddalena, Eddie Murphy, Tom Schumacher, Mireille Soria, Ellen Gurney, Susan Solomon, and more. All of whom I was lucky to learn from whether they knew it or not.

Thanks to my friends at the University of North Georgia for providing me a home away from home to share all I have learned with the next generation of great filmmakers. Many thanks to Bayard Maybank, who served as my agent through

thick and thin, shepherding my career through ups and downs. A heartfelt thanks also to my former writing partner, Chris Parker, who helped me become the writer I am today by filling all the holes I was missing for so long and ultimately driving me to fill them myself.

Many thanks to Michael Wiese, Ken Lee, and their talented team at MWP for taking a chance on me writing my first book and teaching me the literary game. My mother taught me there are stories everywhere. My father taught me I could be anything I wanted. My sister taught me not to be an asshole... and 1,416,302 other things. To them I owe everything.

To my consiglieres, Andrew Firstman, Susan Martin, and Jason James, thank you for being there in the dark and guiding me back to the light. My sincere thanks to the many others who have stood in my corner over the years... Jane Lucker, Adam Rosen, Anna Volkoff, Jeff Marker, David Smith, Joseph Skibell, Paula Vitaris, Eddie Von Mueller, Matthew Bernstein, Donna Little, Mark Roberts, Jim Beach, Nathan Goodman, Walker McKnight, Jenn Lewis, Heather Fracaro, Carter Blanchard, John Welch, Nick Zedlar, Jen Kelley, Robin Henry, Ali Coad, Stephen Weizenecker, Sean Zeid, Melissa Campbell, Bob Hohman, Nicole Watson, Jared Caldwell, and Brian Pollack.

Finally, thanks be to God, The Force, The Universe, for filling my head with all this commotion and, fortunately, a functional way to get it out. I'm sure there's a truckload of other fine folks I am forgetting. Just know that I am here because you were there. And for that I am forever grateful.

APPENDIX

HOMEWORK MOVIES (BY CHAPTER):

1	CONCEPT:	*Die Hard*
2	CHARACTER:	*Braveheart*
3	PLOT:	*Raiders of the Lost Ark*
4	SCENE:	*Kill Bill: Vols. 1 and 2*
5	FORMAT:	*Mission: Impossible*
6	ACTION:	*Lethal Weapon*
7	DIALOGUE:	*Beverly Hills Cop*
8	TRANSITION:	*The Terminator*
9	PROCESS:	*Thelma & Louise*
10	FEEDBACK:	*Top Gun*
11	REWRITING:	*The Bourne Ultimatum*
12	BUSINESS:	*The Matrix*

HOMEWORK ASSIGNMENTS (BY CHAPTER):

1	Write a one-page concept.
2	Write a one-page hero bio.
3	Write a one-page outline.
4	Write a four-page treatment.
5	Write pages 1–5 of your script.
6	Write pages 6–15 of your script.

7   Write pages 16–25 of your script.

8   Write pages 26–35 of your script.

9   Write pages 36–45 of your script.

10 Write pages 46–55 of your script.

11 Rewrite pages 1–55 of your script.

12 Write the rest. You're halfway there!

ADDITIONAL MOVIE AND TV REFERENCES:

A Few Good Men

A League of Their Own

Accountant, The

Air Force One

Anaconda

Arachnophobia

Argo

Avatar

Back to the Future

Butch Cassidy and the Sundance Kid

Cobra

Columbo

Core, The

Days of Thunder

Emperor's New Groove, The

Fast and the Furious, The

Field of Dreams

Game of Thrones

Gone with the Wind

Good Intentions

Harry Potter and the Sorcerer's Stone

Highlander

Home on the Range

In the Line of Fire

Indiana Jones and the Last Crusade
Jaws
Juno
Jurassic Park
Karate Kid, The
Last Action Hero
Last Boy Scout, The
Lilo & Stitch
Logan
Maltese Falcon, The
Memento
Nice Guys, The
Phone Booth
Predator
Rain Man
Rambo
Rocky
Speed
Spirit: Stallion of the Cimarron
Star Trek
Star Wars
Sudden Impact
Swordfish
Transformers
Under Siege
West Wing, The
White House Down
Witness
X-Men

SCREENPLAY SOURCES

Script O' Rama   http://www.script-o-rama.com
Script City   http://scriptcity.com
Simply Scripts   http://www.simplyscripts.com
Script Shark   http://www.scriptshark.com

SCREENPLAY SOFTWARE

Final Draft   http://www.finaldraft.com
Celtx   https://www.celtx.com
Raw Scripts   https://www.rawscripts.com
Fade In   http://www.fadeinpro.com

SCREENPLAY BLOGS

John August   http://johnaugust.com
Terry Rossio   http://www.wordplayer.com
Doug Richardson   http://www.dougrichardson.com
Jen Grisanti   http://www.jengrisanti.com/

SCREENPLAY CREDITS

The talented writers who also worked on the movies Michael did:

Good Intentions   Anthony Stephenson and John Crow

Home on the Range   Will Finn, John Sanford, Michael LaBash,
                       Sam Levine, Mark Kennedy, Robert
                       Lence, Keith Baxter, Mike Kunkel, Jason
                       Lethcoe, Donnie Long, John Norton,
                       Shirley Pierce, Brian Pimental, David
                       Moses Pimental, Ralph Zondag, Davy
                       Liu, Don Hall and Chris Parker

Kronk's New Groove   Tony Leondis, Michael LaBash, Tom,
                       Rogers and Chris Parker

Lilo & Stitch 2: Stitch Has a Glitch	Tony Leondis, Michael LaBash, Eddie Guzellan, Alexa Junge and Chris Parker
Mulan 2	Chris Parker and Roger S. H. Schulman
Spirit: Stallion of the Cimarron	John Fusco and Chris Parker
Vampire in Brooklyn	Chris Parker, Eddie Murphy, Charlie Murphy and Vernon Lynch
101 Dalmatians 2: Patch's London Adventure	Jim Kammerud, Dan Root, Garrett K. Schiff, Brian Smith, Dodie Smith, Temple Matthews and Chris Parker

ABOUT THE AUTHOR

MICHAEL LUCKER

Michael is a writer and director
with twenty-five years' experience
creating film, television, animation, and digital media. He began
his career writing and directing
television commercials in college
at Boston University. Soon after
he landed in Los Angeles working
in production on series and
specials for ABC, NBC, CBS, and HBO before taking a job
as assistant to Steven Spielberg at Amblin Entertainment on
feature films *Indiana Jones and the Last Crusade, Arachnophobia,
Joe Versus the Volcano, Always, Back to the Future II* and *III,*
and *Jurassic Park.* He went on to serve in creative affairs at
Hollywood Pictures where he worked on such movies as
Crimson Tide, Terminal Velocity, Taking Care of Business, and
Straight Talk.

Michael then embarked on a career as a screenwriter,
helping pen more than thirty feature screenplays for such
studios as Paramount, Disney, DreamWorks, Fox, and

Universal, including *Vampire in Brooklyn*, *Home on the Range*, *Good Intentions*, and *Spirit: Stallion of the Cimarron*, which was nominated for an Academy Award in 2002 as best animated feature. He also served as screenwriter on the animated sequels to *Mulan*, *Lilo & Stitch*, *The Emperor's New Groove*, and *101 Dalmatians*. An opportunity to consult to Turner Entertainment took him home to Atlanta in 2007. He went on to launch his own production company, Lucky Dog Filmworks, which now serves as his home for writing and developing film, television, and commercial content. In television, Michael has worked with Animal Planet, Cartoon Network, Travel Channel, History, Discovery, NBC, TBS, TNT, TLC, OWN, DIY, MSNBC and A&E.

A renowned instructor in screenwriting, Michael now lectures at the University of North Georgia, Emory University, and Reinhardt University, and is the founder of Screenwriter School. For more information or to contact him for writing, consulting, or speaking engagements please go to:

www.michaellucker.com

SAVE THE CAT!®
THE LAST BOOK ON SCREENWRITING YOU'LL EVER NEED!

BLAKE SNYDER

BEST SELLER

SAVE THE CAT!
The Last Book On Screenwriting You'll Ever Need!

BLAKE SNYDER

He's made millions of dollars selling screenplays to Hollywood and now screenwriter Blake Snyder tells all. "Save the Cat!®" is just one of Snyder's many ironclad rules for making your ideas more marketable and your script more satisfying — and saleable, including:

- The four elements of every winning logline.
- The seven immutable laws of screenplay physics.
- The 10 genres and why they're important to your movie.
- Why your Hero must serve your idea.
- Mastering the Beats.
- Mastering the Board to create the Perfect Beast.
- How to get back on track with ironclad and proven rules for script repair.

This ultimate insider's guide reveals the secrets that none dare admit, told by a show biz veteran who's proven that you can sell your script if you can save the cat.

"Imagine what would happen in a town where more writers approached screenwriting the way Blake suggests? My weekend read would dramatically improve, both in sellable/producible content and in discovering new writers who understand the craft of storytelling and can be hired on assignment for ideas we already have in house."
> – From the Foreword by Sheila Hanahan Taylor, Vice President,Development at Zide/Perry Entertainment, whose films include *American Pie, Cats and Dogs, Final Destination*

"One of the most comprehensive and insightful how-to's out there. Save the Cat!® *is a must-read for both the novice and the professional screenwriter."*
> – Todd Black, Producer, *The Pursuit of Happyness, The Weather Man, S.W.A.T, Alex and Emma, Antwone Fisher*

"Want to know how to be a successful writer in Hollywood? The answers are here. Blake Snyder has written an insider's book that's informative — and funny, too."
> – David Hoberman, Producer, *The Shaggy Dog* (2005), *Raising Helen, Walking Tall, Bringing Down the House, Monk* (TV)

BLAKE SNYDER, besides selling million-dollar scripts to both Disney and Spielberg, was one of Hollywood's most successful spec screenwriters. Blake's vision continues on *www.blakesnyder.com.*

$19.95 · 216 PAGES · ORDER NUMBER 34RLS · ISBN: 9781932907001

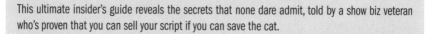

THE WRITER'S JOURNEY
3RD EDITION

MYTHIC STRUCTURE FOR WRITERS

CHRISTOPHER VOGLER

BEST SELLER
OVER 170,000 COPIES SOLD!

See why this book has become an international best seller and a true classic. *The Writer's Journey* explores the powerful relationship between mythology and storytelling in a clear, concise style that's made it required reading for movie executives, screenwriters, playwrights, scholars, and fans of pop culture all over the world.

Both fiction and nonfiction writers will discover a set of useful myth-inspired storytelling paradigms (i.e., "The Hero's Journey") and step-by-step guidelines to plot and character development. Based on the work of Joseph Campbell, *The Writer's Journey* is a must for all writers interested in further developing their craft.

The updated and revised third edition provides new insights and observations from Vogler's ongoing work on mythology's influence on stories, movies, and man himself.

"This book is like having the smartest person in the story meeting come home with you and whisper what to do in your ear as you write a screenplay. Insight for insight, step for step, Chris Vogler takes us through the process of connecting theme to story and making a script come alive."
> – Lynda Obst, Producer, *Sleepless in Seattle, How to Lose a Guy in 10 Days;* Author, *Hello, He Lied*

"This is a book about the stories we write, and perhaps more importantly, the stories we live. It is the most influential work I have yet encountered on the art, nature, and the very purpose of storytelling."
> – Bruce Joel Rubin, Screenwriter, *Stuart Little 2, Deep Impact, Ghost, Jacob's Ladder*

CHRISTOPHER VOGLER is a veteran story consultant for major Hollywood film companies and a respected teacher of filmmakers and writers around the globe. He has influenced the stories of movies from *The Lion King* to *Fight Club* to *The Thin Red Line* and most recently wrote the first installment of *Ravenskull*, a Japanese-style manga or graphic novel. He is the executive producer of the feature film *P.S. Your Cat is Dead* and writer of the animated feature *Jester Till.*

$27.95 · 300 PAGES · ORDER NUMBER 76RLS · ISBN: 193290736x

24 HOURS | **1.800.833.5738** | **WWW.MWP.COM**

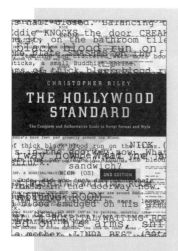

THE HOLLYWOOD STANDARD
2ND EDITION
THE COMPLETE AND AUTHORITATIVE GUIDE TO SCRIPT FORMAT AND STYLE

CHRISTOPHER RILEY

This is the book screenwriter Antwone Fisher (*Antwone Fisher, Tales from the Script*) insists his writing students at UCLA read. This book convinced John August (*Big Fish, Charlie and the Chocolate Factory*) to stop dispensing formatting advice on his popular writing website. His new advice: Consult *The Hollywood Standard*. The book working and aspiring writers keep beside their keyboards and rely on every day. Written by a professional screenwriter whose day job was running the vaunted script shop at Warner Bros., this book is used at USC's School of Cinema, UCLA, and the acclaimed Act One Writing Program in Hollywood, and in screenwriting programs around the world. It is the definitive guide to script format.

The Hollywood Standard describes in clear, vivid prose and hundreds of examples how to format every element of a screenplay or television script. A reference for everyone who writes for the screen, from the novice to the veteran, this is the dictionary of script format, with instructions for formatting everything from the simplest master scene heading to the most complex and challenging musical underwater dream sequence. This new edition includes a quick start guide, plus new chapters on avoiding a dozen deadly formatting mistakes, clarifying the difference between a spec script and production script, and mastering the vital art of proofreading. For the first time, readers will find instructions for formatting instant messages, text messages, email exchanges and caller ID.

"Aspiring writers sometimes wonder why people don't want to read their scripts. Sometimes it's not their story. Sometimes the format distracts. To write a screenplay, you need to learn the science. And this is the best, simplest, easiest to read book to teach you that science. It's the one I recommend to my students at UCLA."

— Antwone Fisher, from the foreword

CHRISTOPHER RILEY is a professional screenwriter working in Hollywood with his wife and writing partner, Kathleen Riley. Together they wrote the 1999 theatrical feature *After the Truth*, a multiple-award-winning German language courtroom thriller. Since then, the husband-wife team has written scripts ranging from legal and political thrillers to action-romances for Touchstone Pictures, Paramount Pictures, Mandalay Television Pictures and Sean Connery's Fountainbridge Films.

In addition to writing, the Rileys train aspiring screenwriters for work in Hollywood and have taught in Los Angeles, Chicago, Washington D.C., New York, and Paris. From 2005 to 2008, the author directed the acclaimed Act One Writing Program in Hollywood.

$24.95 · 208 PAGES · ORDER NUMBER 130RLS · ISBN: 9781932907636

24 HOURS | **1.800.833.5738** | **WWW.MWP.COM**

DIRECTING ACTORS
CREATING MEMORABLE PERFORMANCES
FOR FILM AND TELEVISION

JUDITH WESTON

BEST SELLER
OVER 45,000 COPIES SOLD!

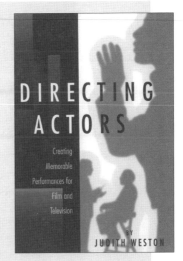

Directing film or television is a high-stakes occupation. It captures your full attention at every moment, calling on you to commit every resource and stretch yourself to the limit. It's the white-water rafting of entertainment jobs. But for many directors, the excitement they feel about a new project tightens into anxiety when it comes to working with actors.

This book provides a method for establishing creative, collaborative relationships with actors, getting the most out of rehearsals, troubleshooting poor performances, giving briefer directions, and much more. It addresses what actors want from a director, what directors do wrong, and constructively analyzes the director-actor relationship.

"Judith Weston is an extraordinarily gifted teacher."
>   – David Chase, Emmy® Award-Winning Writer,
>   Director, and Producer *The Sopranos,*
>   *Northern Exposure, I'll Fly Away*

"I believe that working with Judith's ideas and principles has been the most useful time I've spent preparing for my work. I think that if Judith's book were mandatory reading for all directors, the quality of the director-actor process would be transformed, and better drama would result."
>   – John Patterson, Director
>   *Six Feet Under, CSI: Crime Scene Investigation,*
>   *The Practice, Law and Order*

"I know a great teacher when I find one! Everything in this book is brilliant and original and true."
>   – Polly Platt, Producer, *Bottle Rocket*
>   Executive Producer, *Broadcast News, The War of the Roses*

JUDITH WESTON was a professional actor for 20 years and has taught Acting for Directors for over a decade.

$26.95 · 314 PAGES · ORDER NUMBER 4RLS · ISBN: 0941188248

24 HOURS | **1.800.833.5738** | **WWW.MWP.COM**

FILM DIRECTING: SHOT BY SHOT
VISUALIZING FROM CONCEPT TO SCREEN

STEVEN D. KATZ

BEST SELLER
OVER 190,000 COPIES SOLD!

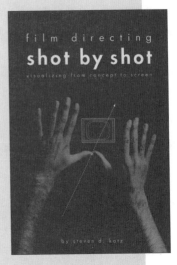

Film Directing: Shot by Shot – with its famous blue cover – is the best-known book on directing and a favorite of professional directors as an on-set quick reference guide.

This international bestseller is a complete catalog of visual techniques and their stylistic implications, enabling working filmmakers to expand their knowledge.

Contains in-depth information on shot composition, staging sequences, visualization tools, framing and composition techniques, camera movement, blocking tracking shots, script analysis, and much more.

Includes over 750 storyboards and illustrations, with never-before-published storyboards from Steven Spielberg's *Empire of the Sun*, Orson Welles' *Citizen Kane*, and Alfred Hitchcock's *The Birds*.

"(To become a director) you have to teach yourself what makes movies good and what makes them bad. John Singleton has been my mentor... he's the one who told me what movies to watch and to read Shot by Shot.*"*
    – Ice Cube, New York Times

"A generous number of photos and superb illustrations accompany each concept, many of the graphics being from Katz' own pen... Film Directing: Shot by Shot *is a feast for the eyes."*
    – Videomaker Magazine

"... demonstrates the visual techniques of filmmaking by defining the process whereby the director converts storyboards into photographed scenes."
    – Back Stage Shoot

"Contains an encyclopedic wealth of information."
    – Millimeter Magazine

STEVEN D. KATZ is also the author of *Film Directing: Cinematic Motion*.

$27.95 · 366 PAGES · ORDER NUMBER 7RLS · ISBN: 0-941188-10-8

24 HOURS | 1.800.833.5738 | WWW.MWP.COM

THE MYTH OF MWP

In a dark time, a light bringer came along, leading the curious and the frustrated to clarity and empowerment. It took the well-guarded secrets out of the hands of the few and made them available to all. It spread a spirit of openness and creative freedom, and built a storehouse of knowledge dedicated to the betterment of the arts.

The essence of the Michael Wiese Productions (MWP) is empowering people who have the burning desire to express themselves creatively. We help them realize their dreams by putting the tools in their hands. We demystify the sometimes secretive worlds of screenwriting, directing, acting, producing, film financing, and other media crafts.

By doing so, we hope to bring forth a realization of 'conscious media' which we define as being positively charged, emphasizing hope and affirming positive values like trust, cooperation, self-empowerment, freedom, and love. Grounded in the deep roots of myth, it aims to be healing both for those who make the art and those who encounter it. It hopes to be transformative for people, opening doors to new possibilities and pulling back veils to reveal hidden worlds.

MWP has built a storehouse of knowledge unequaled in the world, for no other publisher has so many titles on the media arts. Please visit www.mwp.com where you will find many free resources and a 25% discount on our books. Sign up and become part of the wider creative community!

Onward and upward,

Michael Wiese
Publisher/Filmmaker